M. E. von Glehn

Goethe and Mendelssohn

(1821 - 1831)

M. E. von Glehn

Goethe and Mendelssohn
(1821 - 1831)

ISBN/EAN: 9783741101311

Manufactured in Europe, USA, Canada, Australia, Japa

Cover: Foto ©Andreas Hilbeck / pixelio.de

Manufactured and distributed by brebook publishing software (www.brebook.com)

M. E. von Glehn

Goethe and Mendelssohn

GOETHE

AND

MENDELSSOHN.
(1821—1831.)

TRANSLATED, WITH ADDITIONS, FROM THE GERMAN
OF
DR. KARL MENDELSSOHN-BARTHOLDY

BY

M. E. von GLEHN.

WITH PORTRAITS AND FACSIMILE,
AND LETTERS BY MENDELSSOHN OF LATER DATE.

London:
MACMILLAN AND CO.
1872.

CONTENTS.

Zelter, 2; Felix's compositions at twelve years old, 4; Proposed visit to Weimar, 4; His parents' anxiety, 5; Arrival at Weimar, 7; Sees Goethe, 8; Dinner—music—whist—Fanny Mendelssohn's songs, 9; Goethe unbends to Felix, 10, 11; Felix improvises, 12; Minuet in Don Juan and Overture to Figaro, 14; Plays from Autograph of Mozart, 15; and of Beethoven, 16; Conversation about Felix, 19; Goethe's care of him, 21; Romps, *bouts-rimés*, 23; The boy's description of Goethe, 24; Adèle Schopenhauer—Zelter scolded, 25; Goethe's song for Fanny, 27; Felix's judgment—Szymanowska—Riemer, 28; Return to Berlin, 29; Letter from Felix—the *Waldteufel*, 30; the Jacob's-ladder—Adèle's *silhouettes*, 33; more verses by Goethe, 34; and more *silhouettes*,' 35; Sketch by Goethe, 35; Second visit to Weimar, 36; A mother's delight, 37; Saul and David, 38.

Felix fifteen—his fourth opera, 39; Zelter's account, 40; Double-Concerto, 42; Journey to Paris—Cherubini, 42; Felix's judgment on Cherubini, 44; and on music in Paris, 45; Urhahn—Kalkbrenner—Herz, 46; The Opera—Auber's Léocadie, 48; Piccolo, 49; Ignorance of Parisians—Bach and Monsigny, 50; Baillot and Felix's B minor Quartett, 51; Allegro feroce on Paris, 52; Kyrie, 53; Weimar again, 54; Dedication of Quartett to Goethe, 54; Goethe's acknowledgment, 55; Felix translates the "Andria," 56; Foolish critics, 57; Berlin University—Hegel, 59; Goethe's affection for Felix, 61.

Felix starts for Italy, 62; arrives at Weimar, 63; rouses Goethe, 64; Pleasant life, 66; Goethe takes "music lessons," 67; Felix not allowed to go, 68; Conversation in the park—Goethe's

banter, 69; Stendhal—Walter Scott, 70; Schiller, 71; the Grand Duke, 73; the year 1775, 74; Ostade's "Prayer"—Farewell devotions, 76; the Parting, 77; Ottilie's letter, 78.
Munich—Felix's letter, 79; Music parties at Munich—South and North Germany, 81; Rome—ridiculous artists, 83; Goethe's comments, 84; Walpurgis Night, 87; Felix's return through Switzerland, 87; Life in the mountains, 88; Storms, 89; Engelberg—Bach, and Swiss monks, 93; Goethe's birthday, 93; Droll theatre at Lucerne, 95; Schiller's power of production, 96; Goethe's poem on Tell, 97; Goethe and Schiller, 98; Munich—Paris—Goethe's death, 101.

APPENDIX.

LETTERS OF MENDELSSOHN.

I. 1. To Herr Gustav Preusser, June 29, 1842. Plans for Swiss journey, 105; Family greetings, 106.

    2. To his Mother, July 19, 1842. Life and friends at Frankfort, 107; London society, 109; Buckingham Palace, 110; Prince Albert's organ—a royal gift, 111; the Queen's singing, 112; Mendelssohn improvises, 114; Scotch symphony—the parrot, 114; Crossing to Ostend, 115.

    3. To ———, April 2, 1843. Recollections of Paris, 117; Herr Dürrner, 118.

II. 4. To W. Sterndale Bennett, April 3, 1839. Handel's scores, 119; Inquiries as to "Samson," 120; Alternative pieces in "Handel," 121.

    5. To G. A. Macfarren, April 2, 1843. Chevy Chase overture, 122.

    6. To the same, Nov. 20, 1843. Chevy Chase, 125.

    7. To the same, June 6, 1844. Mendelssohn's conscientiousness, 126.

CONTENTS.

8. To the same, Dec. 8, 1844. Performance of "Antigone" at Covent Garden, 128; Chorus-Recitatives, 130; acting of Chorus, 131.

"ISRAEL IN EGYPT."
9. To the Handel Society, March 1, 1845. Subscription of King of Saxony, 134; and King of Prussia, 135; Proofs, 135.
10. To W. Sterndale Bennett, May 26, 1845. Questions as to passages in the autograph of "Israel in Egypt," 136.
11. To G. A. Macfarren, Sept. 28, 1845. Gender of "hautboys," 138; No more alterations, 139; Correction of proofs, 139.
12. To the same, October 1845. Vexatious mistakes of engravers—Organs, 140; Slurs, 141; Suggestions of Council, 143.
13. To the same, Dec. 31, 1845. More suggestions of Council, 145.
14. To the same, April 3, 1846. His own subscription, 146.
15. To the same, Dec. 28, 1845. Final corrections of "Israel," 147; Loyalty to Handel, 148; No Trombones, 149.

III. 16. To the Hofrath Friedrich Rochlitz, Feb. 25, 1835. Thanks for proposed Oratorio-book, 150; Scheme of "St. Paul," 151.
17. To Mr. J. Alfred Novello, April 7, 1838. Prize-fighting in music, 152; Psalm xlii., 153; Cologne Festival, 154.
18. To Herr Anton Zuccalmaglio, Dec. 4, 1839. Thanks for an Opera-book, 154.
19. To Herr Adolf Böttger, Dec. 10, 1841. Legend of "Genoveva," 157.
20. To Professor Wolfgang R. Griepenkerl, Nov. 18, 1844. Opera-book, 158; Shakespeare's "Tempest," 159.

GOETHE
AND
MENDELSSOHN.

GOETHE

AND

MENDELSSOHN.

Most young people need some outlet for their inborn impulses of hero-worship and affection. It is fortunate for them when their enthusiasm is inspired by a true and noble ideal; when their minds can gain force and elevation from the examples of great men, rising like constellations above the horizon of their own time.

The opportunities which Felix Mendelssohn enjoyed as a boy, of seeing and knowing Goethe in his own house, gave an impulse to his whole life. Goethe's living presence strengthened and fostered that love for perfection, and that dislike for everything mean and morbid, which always distinguished him.

The meeting was brought about by Zelter, an original in every sense of the word. Whatever Zelter did, he did by himself alone. We know from his autobiography* that though forced by his father to work at the mason's trade, yet, both as apprentice and journeyman, he pursued music unceasingly till he had thoroughly acquired the art, never allowing himself to be discouraged by the depreciatory remarks of professional musicians, such as Kirnberger, who told him to his face that "while an ordinary workman is always respectable, there is nothing more pitiable than an ordinary artist, such as you will be."

Like most autocrats, Zelter had a very positive and rough manner of his own, and his plain speaking and rudeness were proverbial among the artists of Berlin. There was some-

* Carl Friedrich Zelter, eine Lebenschreibung. Nach autobiographischen Manuscripten bearbeitet von Dr. Wilhelm Rintel. Berlin, 1861.

thing rigid, stubborn, and rough-hewn about him, a native force which nothing but the wonderfully harmonious personality of Goethe could have softened. From the moment of his reading "Werther" he was filled with a deep sympathy and attraction for the man whose knowledge of human nature had enabled him to give such a work to the world; and after he had become personally acquainted with him there was no one who clung with truer devotion to Goethe. The correspondence between the two is a lasting memorial of the union of characteristic force and true friendship.

Zelter speaks of the artistic efforts of the Berliners, describes the progress of the "Sing-Akademie," and at an early period in the correspondence draws the attention of the great art-patron at Weimar to Felix Mendelssohn, the most gifted of his pupils.

In a letter of the 26th October, 1821, he thus announces to his friend his proposed visit to Weimar: "I want to show your face to my Doris, and my best pupil, before I leave the world, though I certainly mean to hold out in it as long as possible. The boy is good and pretty, lively and obedient."

Felix was then only twelve years old, but for that age he had already displayed extraordinary musical productivity. He had written two operas, and nearly finished a third; had composed for the Sing-Akademie a Psalm in four and five parts with a grand double fugue; as well as six symphonies, a quartett for piano and strings, a cantata, six fugues for pianoforte, and a number of studies, sonatas, and songs.

"Just fancy," says his mother, writing to her sister-in-law, Henriette Mendelssohn, in Paris, "that the little wretch is to have the good luck of going to Weimar with Zelter for a short time. He wants to show him to Goethe, and is to take him there next week after they have been to the exhibition of Schadow's picture of

Luther at Wittenberg. You can imagine what it costs me to part from the dear child, even for a few weeks. But I consider it such an advantage for him to be introduced to Goethe, to live under the same roof with him, and enjoy the blessing of so great a man. I am also glad of this little journey as a change for him; for his impulsiveness sometimes makes him work harder than he ought to at his age."

It may easily be understood how much the boy was exhorted to make the most of the rare opportunity thus afforded him. " Keep your wits about you," writes his father. " Every time I write to you, my dear boy, I shall remind you to keep a strict watch over yourself; to sit properly and behave nicely, especially at dinner; to speak distinctly and suitably, and try as much as possible to express yourself to the point. I know what a good fellow you are, and therefore think it hardly necessary to remind you to be good and modest, and obedient to your fatherly friend and guide, and not to forget often to think affectionately of us."

His mother writes: "If I could but be a little mouse so as to watch my dear Felix while he's away, and see how he comports himself as an independent youth. Mind you snap up every word that Goethe says: I want to know all about him."

Nor could his elder sister, Fanny, resist adding her exhortations: "When you are with Goethe, I advise you to open your eyes and ears wide; and after you come home, if you can't repeat every word that fell from his mouth, I will have nothing more to do with you. It's better for us to lose you for a little, that during that time you may lay up the most precious recollections for your future life."

The reports which the young traveller sent home to these anxious monitors exhibit a peculiar mixture of observation with the happy ingenuousness of a child. He describes the beautiful arrangement of Goethe's house; the pleasant "Salve" which greeted him on the threshold of the door leading to the chief apartment; the statues on the steps and in the lobby, which suggested Greece, the dreamland of the poet. No doubt the boy's heart beat as he trod the sacred threshold.

"Now, stop and listen, all of you," he writes on the 6th November. "To-day is Tuesday. On Sunday, the sun of Weimar—Goethe—arrived. In the morning we went to church, and they gave us half of Handel's 100th Psalm. (The organ is large, but weak; the Marien-organ,* small as it is, is much more powerful. This one has 50 stops.)

"Afterwards I went to the 'Elephant,' where I sketched the house of Lucas Cranach. Two hours afterwards Professor Zelter came and said, 'Goethe has come,—the old gentleman's come!'

* The organ of the Marien-Kirche at Berlin.

and in a minute we were down the steps and in Goethe's house. He was in the garden, and was just coming round a corner. Isn't it strange, dear father? that was exactly how you met him. He is very kind, but I don't think any of the pictures are like him.

"He was looking over his collection of petrifactions, which his son had arranged for him, and kept saying, 'Hm, hm! I am very much pleased.' After that I stayed in the garden with him and Professor Zelter for half an hour. Then came dinner. One would never take him for seventy-three, but for fifty. After dinner Fräulein Ulrike, the sister of Frau von Goethe, asked for a kiss, and I did the same. Every morning I get a kiss from the author of 'Faust' and 'Werther,' and every afternoon two kisses from my friend and father Goethe. Think of that! (In Leipsic I went several times through Auerbach's curious courtyard, a great passage, like many others in Leipsic, filled with shops and people, and shut in by houses six or seven stories high. On the market-place there is actually one of nine stories.)

"But where am I wandering to! After dinner I played to Goethe for two hours and more, partly Bach fugues, and partly extempore. In the evening they played whist, and Professor Zelter, who played with them at first, said, 'Whist means that you are to hold your tongue!' What a good saying! We had supper all together, even Goethe too, though generally he never eats anything in the evening. Now, my dear coughing Fanny!* yesterday morning I took your songs to Frau von Goethe, who has a pretty voice. She is going to sing them to the old gentleman. I told him that you had written some, and asked if he would hear them. He said, 'Yes, yes, very willingly.' Frau von Goethe liked them very

* This probably refers to a supposed habit of Fanny Mendelssohn's, of criticising her brother's compositions by coughing. After telling her of the honour and kindness shown him, he thus jokingly challenges her disapproval.

much, which is a good omen. He is to hear them to-day or to-morrow. I am so sorry that I shall not see Lipinski again."

It is easy to see that Felix soon got over the constraint of the first acquaintance, and made himself at home in the house of the man whom others approached with the greatest deference.

The descriptions which Goethe's contemporaries give of his appearance—the solemn, slow gait, the powerful features, the lofty brow on which Apollo had set his seal of strength and wisdom, the abundant grey hair, the deep voice and measured speech, all convey an impression of stately dignity. Even Zelter, who usually despised all outward forms, used to appear at Goethe's in the fullest dress; that is to say, short black silk breeches, silk stockings, and shoes with great silver buckles, a costume long out of fashion, and supposed to bear the stamp of peculiar solemnity. Goethe himself admitted that he reserved a certain indifference of manner for strangers who came to visit him, and it is well known how cold and repelling he was to Carl Maria von Weber. But for the "little Berliner" he laid aside all his ministerial dignity, and stroked and patted his head with such fatherly tenderness, that the boy soon lost all bashfulness, and gave way to his tremendous spirits in all their youthful freshness. It was evident that Goethe felt quite as much personal attraction for the boy as interest in his music. At the first party which Goethe gave for the Berliners, he amused himself with making a trial of Felix's talent before all the company. "My friend Zelter," he said to Rellstab,* "has brought his little pupil to see me; we are to have a trial of his musical powers, but he is extraordinarily talented in other ways as well. You know the doctrine of tempera-

---

* See Rellstab's *Aus meinem Leben*, Berlin, 1861, vol. ii. chapter 11.—" Mendelssohn im Goetheschen Haus."

ments; everyone has all the four in him, only in different proportions. Well, this boy, I should say, possesses the smallest possible modicum of the phlegmatic, and the maximum of the opposite quality."

The first test to which Goethe put the young artist was to make him improvise on a theme furnished by Zelter. Zelter sat down to the piano, and with his stiff, cramped fingers played a very simple tune in triplets, "Ich träumte einst von Hannchen," as tame and trivial an air as need be. Felix played it through after him, and the next minute went off into the wildest allegro, transforming the simple melody into a passionate figure, which he took now in the bass, now in the upper part, weaving all manner of new and beautiful thoughts into it in the boldest style. Everybody was in astonishment, as the small childish fingers worked away at the great chords, mastering the most difficult combinations, and evolving the most surprising contrapuntal passages out of a stream of harmonies, though certainly without paying much regard to the melody.

It was one of Zelter's principles to be very chary of praise; his aim being to save his pupil from conceit and over-estimation of his own powers — "those cursed enemies of all artistic progress," as he called them. No sooner therefore had Felix finished than he said, in a tone of the most complete indifference, like an old pedagogue bent on spoiling the boy's brilliant success, "What hobgoblins and dragons have you been dreaming about, to drive you along in that helter-skelter fashion!"

Goethe saw his object, and taking the head of the little artist in his two hands, and caressing it, said in a playful way: "But you won't get off with that; you must play more before we can quite believe in you." So Felix had to play Bach fugues, of which Goethe was particularly fond; then he asked for a minuet, upon which the boy cried out with flashing eyes, "Shall I play you the most beautiful one in the whole world?" and played the Minuet from Don Juan.

Goethe stood by the piano listening attentively, and his eyes sparkling with pleasure. After the Minuet he asked for the Overture, but this the little player refused on the spot, declaring, "It can't be played as it is written, and it wouldn't be right to alter it in the least." He offered, however, to play the Overture to Figaro instead, and acquitted himself of the task with so much confidence and ease, rendering the orchestral effects so completely, bringing out so many delicate touches in the instrumentation by his manner of playing, and giving each part its due prominence, that the effect was overpowering. Goethe became more and more genial and lively, and tried all sorts of tricks and jokes on his little guest.

"So far," said he, "you have only played me what you knew before; now we will see if you can play something that you don't know." He went out, and returned with a number of sheets of written music. "Here," said he, "are some things out of my collection of manuscripts. Now we will put you to the test; see if you can play that:" and he placed on the desk a sheet of music, in clear but very small writing. It was an autograph of Mozart's. The boy solved the task as readily as if he had known the piece by heart for years. "That's nothing," said Goethe, as everybody was applauding loudly; "other people can read that too; but now I am going to give you something in which you will break down. So take care!" And with this joking threat he got out another manuscript and put it on the desk. This one did indeed look strange. It was difficult to say whether it was music at all, or merely a sheet of ruled paper bespattered with ink and smudged all over. Felix burst out laughing, and exclaimed,

"What writing! how is it possible to read that?" But suddenly he became serious; for when Goethe asked, "Now guess *who* wrote that!" Zelter, looking over the boy's shoulder as he sat at the piano, called out: "Why, it's Beethoven's writing;[*] one can see that a mile off. He always writes as if he used a broomstick, and then wiped his sleeve over the wet ink. I have several manuscripts of his; they are soon recognized."

Felix kept his eyes reverently fixed on the paper; and his whole face glowed with excitement, as out of the chaos of words and notes, scratched out, smudged, interlined, and written over one another, he brought to light some lofty thought of beauty, or some deep noble senti-

[*] Goethe had made acquaintance with Beethoven at Töplitz, but had not learned to appreciate his "uncontrolled personality." "His talent excited my astonishment, but unfortunately his personality is entirely uncontrolled; he is perfectly welcome to think the world detestable, but by that means he does not make it more enjoyable for himself or for others." (Letter to Zelter, Carlsbad, Sept. 2, 1812.)

F. Mendelssohn

From a Sketch taken in or about 1821

ment. But Goethe, anxious to make the test a really severe one, left him no time to consider, but kept urging him on:—"You see, didn't I tell you that you would break down? Now try, and show what you can do." Felix began to play at once. It was a simple song, but to distinguish the right notes, among those that had been scratched out and half smeared out, required a rare quickness and sharpness of perception. At the first reading Felix had often to point laughingly with his finger to the right note which was to be found in quite another place; and many a mistake had to be corrected with a hurried "No, that's it." But at the end he said, "Now I will play it to you," and the second time there was not a single wrong note. "That's Beethoven," he exclaimed once as he came upon a phrase which seemed to him to bear the stamp of the composer's individuality; "that is quite Beethoven : I should have known him by that." With this trial Goethe let him off. He concealed his praise under pleasant banter—"*Here* you broke down, you know, and *here* you were not safe;" but it was easy to see what a keen artistic pleasure he took in the boy's triumph.

A day or two after, when the youthful composer's first quartett * had been performed, and Felix himself, after playing the pianoforte part, had run off into the garden, Goethe remarked to the other players : † "Musical prodigies, as far as mere technical execution goes, are probably no longer so rare : but what this little man can do in extemporizing and playing at sight, borders on the miraculous, and I could not have believed it possible at so early an age."

"And yet you heard Mozart in his seventh year at Frankfort?" said Zelter.

"Yes," answered Goethe ; "at that time I myself

* In B minor, Op. 3. Afterwards dedicated to Goethe. See page 54.

† See Prof. Lobe's Reminiscences in the *Gartenlaube* for 1867, No. 1. Also, by the same, *Consonanzen und Dissonanzen;* Leipsic, 1869.

had only just reached my twelfth year, and was certainly, like all the rest of the world, immensely astonished at his extraordinary execution; but what your pupil already accomplishes, bears the same relation to the Mozart of that time, that the cultivated talk of a grown-up person does to the prattle of a child."

The conversation turned upon the young artist's talent for composition. The musicians hoped that as Felix's ideas were more independent than those of Mozart at the same age, a most brilliant future might be predicted for him.

"May it be so," said Goethe. "But who can tell in what manner a mind may ultimately unfold itself? One sees so much talent, full of the highest promise, take a false direction, and disappoint the most sanguine expectations! However, from this fate our young genius will be preserved by the master whom good fortune has provided him with in Zelter."

Zelter would not let these words pass unquestioned. "True," he observed; "I feel my responsibility about the boy, and besides his own voluntary work I keep him seriously to the point with severe studies in counterpoint, but it will not be long before he escapes from my discipline. Even now he has learned almost everything that is essential; and once free, it will then first be seen what his actual bent will be."

"Yes, and above all," remarked Goethe, "the influence of a teacher is always problematical. That which constitutes the real greatness and individuality of an artist, must be produced out of himself alone. To what teachers did Rafaelle, Michel Angelo, Haydn, Mozart, and all the great masters owe their immortal creations?"

With all his fatherly tenderness for the "little Berliner" one sees how free from bias the poet was in his judgment of him. He specially inquired of Zelter how Felix was educated at Berlin, and whether, according to Berlin fashion, he was not too much coddled. He did not like to see so much fuss made with the boy by all the company. He forbade him to go over to Jena for a concert which had been got up by the students there; in fact, he was no great friend to concerts or music in a general way; and once at court, when a pianoforte player was in the middle of a very long sonata, he got up, and, to the horror of all the throng of court ladies and gentlemen, said, "If it lasts three minutes longer, I confess everything."

During his stay at Weimar, Felix played much more than usual, often from six to eight hours a day; he played before the Grand Duke and Grand Duchess of Russia, and the Princesses; he even had the "audacity," as he writes to his mother, to improvise before all the court, and in presence of Hummel. His G minor sonata* was very much praised by both

---

* Begun "18th June, 1820;" finished "18th August, 1821." Recently published as Opus 105.—*Trans.*

the Grand Duke and Hummel. The chief lady-in-waiting of the Grand Duchess began to make a drawing of him, and the ladies were all so absurd about him that Goethe complained to Zelter, "These women here are doing all they can to spoil the boy for me." But one day, when Felix had been ordered to play at court, he was kept outside in the antechamber of the Belvedere; the servants would not let him pass: so at last, instead of playing, he went off to Weimar in a pet, and left the court to wait for him. For which he doubtless underwent a paternal lecture from the Herr Geheimrath.

The little Berliner had in a short time become the favourite of the whole Goethe family. Often when sitting at the piano, weaving into one long fantasia all manner of favourite airs, such as "Treibt der Champagner," Eberwein's songs, Körner's "Treuen Tod," the Triangle Waltz (in that Philhellenic time of course called the "Ipsilantiwalzer"), he would jump up in the middle to have a good chase round the room with the younger ladies. Once he teased one of the ladies-in-waiting with a bellows, which he had picked up somewhere near the fireplace, and maliciously directed at her curls—and yet no one was ever angry with him. "If you think I am little Zaches," he writes to his sister Fanny at Berlin, "then Doris must be Rosabelverde, for it is she that curbs me, ungovernable steed that I am."

It was impossible at Weimar to escape the atmosphere of poetry, and so round-games of rhymes formed part of the day's amusements; Felix and the ladies had many a contest over *bouts rimés*, often ending with a noisy appeal to the great master himself to arbitrate on their doggrel. Goethe entered heartily into the uproarious spirits of the young people, and was very loth to let the Berliners go; and when at the end of a fortnight Zelter began to talk of going home, he seriously reprimanded him.

"Every afternoon," says Felix, "Goethe opens the Streicher piano * with these words, 'I have not heard you at all to-day, so you must make a little noise for me.' Then he sits down by me, and when I have finished (generally improvising) I beg for a kiss, or else I take one. You can have no conception of his goodness and kindness, nor of the quantity of minerals, busts, engravings, statuettes, and large drawings which this Pole-star of poets has in his possession. That he has an imposing figure, I cannot see; he is really not much bigger than my father. But his look, his language, his name, they are imposing. His voice has an enormous

* "By the thoughtful care of our long-tried friend, Hofrath Rochlitz, a most carefully tested Streicher piano arrived from Leipsic; very fortunately; for soon afterwards Zelter brought us his astonishing and remarkable pupil Felix Mendelssohn, with whose marvellous talent we should never have become acquainted, without the help of such a 'Mechanik.'"—*Tag und Jahreshefte.*

sound in it, and he can shout like ten thousand fighting men. His hair is not yet white, his walk is steady, and his manner of speaking gentle.

"Zelter wanted to go to Jena on Tuesday, and from there on to Leipsic. On Saturday, Adèle Schopenhauer came to us, and, contrary to his custom, Goethe stayed the whole evening. The conversation turned upon our departure, and Adèle proposed that we should all go and throw ourselves at Professor Zelter's feet and implore for a few days' grace. He was dragged into the room, and then Goethe burst out with his thundering voice, scolded Professor Zelter for wanting to take us away to the old nest, commanded him to be silent, to obey without a word, to leave me here, to go to Jena alone and then come back — in fact he so completely drove him into a corner that he will do everything that Goethe wishes. After this Goethe was assailed by everybody with kisses on his mouth and hands, and whoever could not reach these, stroked and kissed his shoulders; if he had not been at home, I think we should have taken him to his house, as the Roman people did Cicero after the first Catiline oration. Fräulein Ulrike also had thrown herself upon his neck, and as he is making love to her, and she is very pretty, the effect of the whole was capital."

So it was decided to lengthen the visit, and to go on making music, writing verses, and enjoying happy days.

"When Goethe says to me, 'My little one, to-morrow there is a party, and you must play for us,' how can I possibly say No? Goethe has heard 'Ach wer bringt die schönen Tage,' and said to me, 'I say, that is a very pretty song.'"*

---

* Letter of the 14th November to his parents. The allusion is to Fanny Mendelssohn's setting of this poem, hitherto unpublished, and not to be confounded with my father's later well-known composition (Op. 99, No. 1).

Felix had told him that his sister Fanny wanted some words to set to music; so one day Goethe came with a poem written expressly for her, saying to Zelter, as he handed it to him, "Give this to the dear child." It ran thus:

AN DIE ENTFERNTE.

Wenn ich mir in stiller Seele
  Singe leise Lieder vor:
Wie ich fühle, dass sie fehle,
  Die ich einzig auserkor.
Möcht ich hoffen, dass sie sänge
  Was ich ihr so gern vertraut;
Ach! aus dieser Brust und Enge
  Drängen frohe Lieder laut.*

When in silence of the soul,
  Softly to myself I sing,
How I miss her whom my whole
  Heart hath set o'er everything!
Would she sing what in her ear
  My full heart would fain be telling,
From this breast, so vainly swelling,
  Songs would break forth glad and clear.

---

* Goethe's autograph is now in the possession of Fanny's son Sebastian Hensel, to whom I am indebted for the above.

However, with all her veneration for the manuscript, Fanny never attempted to compose it.

It is characteristic of the boy that though only twelve, and full of reverence for the great poet, he should never have allowed his judgement to be biassed. Of Mdlle. Szymanowska, a Polish pianoforte player, whom Goethe used to praise enthusiastically, he writes: "People set the Szymanowska above Hummel. They have confused her pretty face with her not-pretty playing." When he had to dine with Goethe's friend Riemer, he said it gave him "quite a Greek feeling;" and he described the great lexicographer with due respect as follows: "He seems to thrive on the making of Lexicons. He is stout and fat, and as shiny as a priest or a full moon." If Goethe had heard these and similar expressions of his little Berlin guest, they would no doubt have confirmed his opinion of the Berliners, which he himself thus pronounced to Eckermann: "From all that I see,

I gather that the Berliners as a class are such a forward set, that delicacy is thrown away on them; one must have one's eyes wide open and be even a little rude to keep above water."*
At dessert he gave his young friend as a parting gift a little red box, which Felix, to his delight, found to contain a silver medal with the portrait of the poet by Borry.

When the young traveller returned to Berlin, after all these impressions and excitements, he seemed ten times more lively than ever. "The first day," writes his mother, "he was really like a volcano, quite bursting with fun and spirits. Zelter had charged him to speak slowly and distinctly, but you can fancy how such an injunction would act on his tremendous excitability. Their absence grew from a fortnight to four weeks, of which the sixteen days that he spent in Goethe's house will always be memorable to him. Zelter and Doris

* Conversation of 4th December, 1823.

could not talk enough about the sensation he created in Weimar."

The approach of Christmas gave Felix the opportunity of recalling himself to the memory of his Weimar friends in an amusing way. At Ottilie's wish he sent his playfellows Wolf and Walter a kind of rattle (called in Germany a *Waldteufel*—that is, a Wood-spirit), a favourite toy of the Berlin street-boys; and he accompanied his present with the following letter:—

"A 'WALDTEUFEL.' *

"Here is the 'Waldteufel.' You command—and it is done. Will you be so good as to give it to my dear little playfellow as a small Christmas present. But I rather advise you to taboo this droning little brute, for the sound of him in a room is most excruciating; out of

---

* Communicated by Professor Nohl from the original in the Hofbibliothek at Carlsruhe.

doors, at the Berlin Christmas fair, where you see and hear the noisy things by hundreds, the clatter is more bearable. I do so wish (out of pure selfishness) you were here, and could see it all with your own eyes. Walter would be delighted with the fair, the lights, the toys, and the racket, and hubbub, and din, and screaming, of the 'Waldteufel' and the children. And if the Herr Kammerrath wants to be sickened of the famous Ypsilanti, he had better come to Berlin and go to the fair, where one can hear it, with or without variations. But to him the best part of all the fun would be the happy faces wherever you go, both of givers and receivers.

"You would enjoy the fair this year, for it is most splendid, and up to. to-day, the 20th of December, we have not had more than one degree of frost.

"So much for the Berlin Christmas fair.

"Volti Subito.

"*What is all Weimar about?*
"*What an important question!*

"It was my father's birthday on the 11th. We gave him as much as we could. All our friends gave him presents. But one present, of course, surpassed all the rest. The Herr Geheimrath's letter arrived on that day. As to his sometimes in the afternoons making a little motion with his head, I can hardly flatter myself; it would be far too great an honour for my strumming, and good as he is, I can scarcely believe it. Do you think I might venture to remind him of the leaf he promised for my book?

"A thousand greetings to Miss Adèle.* We

---

* Adèle Schopenhauer had a wonderful talent for cutting out paper. She had made a "Jacob's ladder" for Felix; that is to say, she cut out in black paper two staves of music with angels floating up and down them. Beneath the ladder thus formed there were clouds, and beneath these a sleeping figure, with its face turned upwards. The whole was mounted on pink paper, and on the back was written: "Jacob, in his dream, saw a ladder reaching up to heaven, with angels ascending

all look forward to the witches-broom * as much as to Christmas-eve, if I may make use of this stale and unpoetical simile. Everybody who comes here has to see the 'Ladder' † (and consequently admire it, and consequently envy me). Varnhagen saw it the other day, and was rather taken aback by it. However, in a few days he brought my sister one, which is to be a *pendant* to yours. It is very delicate, like everything that he cuts out, but in the grouping, and more especially the idea, it is far, far behind yours.

and descending on it; the ladder is still standing upon earth, and the ascending and descending angels are the notes which carry the sounds up to heaven." Varnhagen possessed the same talent as Adèle, and was incited by her masterpiece to cut out a basket of flowers with fairies hovering around it, for Fanny Mendelssohn.

* Another of Adèle Schopenhauer's *silhouettes*,—described on page 34.

† To understand the point of the allusion to the Jacob's ladder, it may be well to explain that the German for the Scale is "Tonleiter," literally a "ladder of sound."—*Trans.*

"Please remember me to Herr and Madame Eberwein, and give my love to the Wolf.

"Your faithful

"F. Mendelssohn."

The promised leaf for the album was not long in arriving. Adèle Schopenhauer and Goethe united to give their little Berlin friend a pleasant surprise. Adèle had cut out in her best style, in pink paper, a winged hobby-horse in the shape of a witches-broom, bestridden by a little elf, crowned and decked with flowers; and underneath, Goethe had written the following lines in the most formal hand:—

"Wenn über die ernste Partitur
Quer Steckenpferdchen reiten,
Nur zu auf weiter Töne Flur,
Wirst Manchem Lust bereiten,
Wie du's gethan mit Lieb' und Glück.
Wir wünschen Dich allesammt zurück.

GOETHE.

WEIMAR, *den 20ten Januar,* 1822."

When up the score and down again
Small hobby-horses ride,

> Away o'er music's wide domain
> Fresh pleasure you'll provide,
> As you have done with loving gain.
> We all here wish you back again.

In the autograph of the above, the signature "Goethe" alone is in a bold free hand. With Psyche's hobby-horse there is a second *silhouette* by Adèle—a figure elaborately got up, in dress-coat, shirt-frill, and knee-breeches, hat in hand, making a solemn low bow: the profile is Goethe's, and on the back of his neck is perched a little winged genius, with hands out, strumming upon his head. The two *silhouettes*, with the autograph of the verses and the "Jacob's ladder," are still in my father's album, together with the autograph of the lines, "Zwar die vier und zwanzig Ritter," as far as "besonders aber eine, welche wir zu segnen kamen," and the manuscript (referred to below) from the second part of Faust: also a pen-and-ink sketch by Goethe, representing a Greek temple, with a figure holding a lyre descending the steps. The temple recalls the singular building which he erected in the park at Weimar. Close by is the open sea, with the peaks of an island rising in the distance. On the grass before the temple is a Greek woman in deep meditation.

The old poet's interest in the young musician continued without abatement. He writes to Zelter on the 5th of February, 1822: "Say something nice to Felix from me, and also to his parents. Since your departure my piano remains dumb; a single attempt to awaken it almost turned out a failure."

In the autumn of 1822 Felix repeated his visit, this time in company with his sister Fanny and his parents, who thus had the pleasure of seeing with their own eyes how quickly and how surely their son had won the hearts of all.

"In the Goethes and Schopenhauers we have made the most delightful and never-to-be-forgotten acquaintances," writes his mother. "With a true mother's pleasure I saw how immensely beloved Felix had made himself amongst these superior people, and his happy parents are proud to owe to him the wonderful kindness with which they were received. Goethe, the distinguished, exalted Minister, around whose head dignity, renown, poetic fame, genius, and distinction of every kind form a dazzling crown of glory, and before whom common mortals tremble, is so sweet and kind-hearted and so like a father to the boy, that it is only with the deepest gratitude and most joyful emotion that I can recall these delightful times. He talked for hours with my husband about Felix, and earnestly begged to have him again for a still longer visit; his eyes dwelt on him with evident satisfaction, and his gravity was turned into gaiety when he had been improvising to his satisfaction. As he does not care for ordinary music, his piano had remained untouched during Felix's absence, but as he opened it for him he said, 'Come and awaken for me all the winged * spirits which have so long been slumbering here.' And another time: 'You are my David, and if I am ever ill and sad, you must banish my bad dreams by your playing; I shall never throw my spear at you, as Saul did.' Isn't that too touching from an old man of seventy-three? Felix, who in a general way seems rather indifferent to praise, is, with good reason, proud of the favour which Goethe shows him, and this feeling can only elevate and improve him. He was also very friendly and condescending to Fanny; she had to play a good deal of Bach to him, and he was extremely pleased with those of his songs which she had composed; in fact, it is always a great delight to him to see his things set to music."

* "Geflügelte Geister." There is a play in the words here which cannot well be rendered into English, "Flügel" being the German word for a piano as well as for a wing.—*Trans.*

In the succeeding years also, Zelter had the satisfaction of being able to make gratifying reports to Goethe of Felix's progress. "My Felix," he writes on the 11th of March, 1823, "has entered upon his fifteenth year. He grows under my very eyes. His wonderful pianoforte playing I may consider as quite a thing apart. He might also become a great violin player. The second act of his fourth opera is finished. In everything he gains, and even force and power are now hardly wanting; everything comes from within him, and the external things of the day only affect him externally. Imagine my joy, if we survive, to see the boy living in the fulfilment of all that his childhood gives promise of!"

"Yesterday," he reports on the 8th of February, 1824, "we gave a complete performance, with dialogue, of Felix's fourth opera.* There are

---

* The fourth opera was "Die beiden Neffen, oder Der Onkel aus Boston. Oper in 3 Acten"—still in manuscript.

three acts and two ballets, filling up about an hour and a half. The work met with a very favourable reception. I cannot get over my astonishment at the enormous strides which this boy of fifteen makes. Novelty, beauty, individuality, originality, all alike are to be found in him,—genius, fluency, repose, harmony, completeness, dramatic power, and the solidity of an experienced hand. His instrumentation is interesting; not overpowering or fatiguing, and yet not mere accompaniment. The musicians like playing his music, and yet it is not exactly easy. Now and then a familiar idea comes and passes on again, not as if borrowed, but, on the contrary, fit and proper for its place. Gaiety, spirit without flurry, tenderness, finish, love, passion, and innocence.—The Overture is a singular thing. Imagine a painter flinging a dab of colour on his canvas and then working it about with fingers and brushes till at last a group emerges, and you look at it with fresh wonder, and only see that it must be true because there it is. No doubt I am talking like an old grandfather bent on spoiling his grandchild. But I know what I say, and say nothing which I can't prove. And my first proof is public approval, especially that of the players and singers; because it is easy to discover whether their fingers and throats are set in motion by coldness and ill-will, or love and pleasure. You must surely understand this. Just as a writer who speaks to the heart is sure to please, so is a composer who gives the player something which he can not only play and enjoy himself, but make others enjoy too. This speaks for itself.—I may hope that you will take my account of Felix's progress as grist to my own mill.

"You know the misery of these schools even better than I do: great aims, little talent, enormous means, and all for nothing. These are the evils; and so one ought indeed to be glad to find some one who does what he can, and is always ready for every emergency."

In a letter of the 26th of December, 1824, he says: "To-day we are to hear my Felix's latest double Concerto.* The boy is now well rooted, and gives promise of growing into a healthy tree. His individuality becomes more and more apparent, and blends itself so well with the spirit of the age, that it seems to come out of it like a bird from the egg."

In the spring of 1825, Felix went to Paris with his father to consult Cherubini as to making music his vocation. Cherubini had long been a perfect terror to the artists of Paris, and everyone trembled at his bitter sarcasms. Halévy had fairly frightened the new arrivals by telling them that there were days when it was impossible to extract anything from him. To a young musician who played to

* In E major, for two pianos and orchestra. This work, like the former one in A flat, still remains in manuscript.

him, he said: "Do you perhaps paint well?" and to another: "Vous ne ferez jamais rien!" When Halévy showed him anything of his own it was a sure sign of its being especially good if Cherubini said nothing and made no faces. Once, and once only, when Halévy had played his opera "La Juive" to him, did the spiteful old Maestro deign a remark: "C'est bien, mais c'est trop long; il faut couper."

Felix had just finished his B minor quartett for piano and strings, and intended to dedicate it to Goethe. It is easy to imagine the excitement of the Parisians when, after a very poor performance by French artists, Cherubini went up to Felix smiling and nodding. He then turned to the bystanders and said: "Ce garçon est riche; il fera bien; il fait même déjà bien, mais il dépense trop de son argent, il met trop d'étoffe dans son habit." Everyone declared that such a thing was unheard of, especially as Cherubini afterwards added, "Je lui parlerai, alors il fera bien." Halévy was not present at the time, and absolutely refused to believe that Cherubini could have so spoken to a young musician. To us, however, it seems natural enough for one who had received Goethe's blessing, not to be afraid of Cherubini.

The opinions which the boy expressed on the dreaded Maestro and on the general state of music in Paris, show a decided independence of mind and real originality. He compares Cherubini to an extinct volcano, still throwing out occasional flashes and sparks, but quite covered with ashes and stones. In the "Kyrie" which he wrote for Cherubini during his stay in Paris, he actually ventured to parody the style of the terrible old Maestro himself.

"Clever fellow!" says Zelter; "he has contrived to compose the piece in a style which, though possibly not the right one, is just the one which Cherubini was groping after, and, unless I am mistaken, has not found."

Felix felt in his heart that his vocation was to be a German artist; and the conviction made him shrink from the excitement of Paris, and blame the want of serious musical feeling and of true enthusiasm for the art, which prevailed among the French musicians.

"I had hoped," says he, "to find this the native home of music, musicians, and musical taste; but, upon my word, it is nothing of the kind. The *salons*, though I did not expect much from them, are wearisome; people care only for trivial, showy music, and won't put up with anything serious or solid. The orchestras (I have heard those of the Opera and the Académie Royale) are very good, but by no means perfect; and lastly, the musicians themselves are either dried up, or else do nothing but abuse Paris and the Parisians.

"At the concert at Tremont last Sunday I heard

Urhahn * play some variations on the viola. He tunes it differently to the usual way, that is to say, fc, fc. This is very effective the first time you hear it, but still it is a bad plan, for the instrument loses the depth of the viola without gaining the acuteness of the violin, while it is obviously only available in F major, or at best C major. After this Kalkbrenner played a new sextett of his own in A minor. The piano has quite the leading part, and the clarinet, cello, and double-bass merely accompany. There are some pretty

---

* A friend has kindly given me the following information:—
"Urhahn was the principal viola player at the Grand Opéra. He was my godfather, a great and dear friend of my parents, a profound musician, and the greatest original imaginable. His originality showed itself in an excess of piety; while playing the Soli in the ballet of the Grand Opéra he never would look at the ballet dancers, even when Habeneck, the conductor, bade him do so for the sake of the *ensemble*. He was ascetic in the full sense of the word, and would for eight or ten days live on radishes and bread and butter to get rid of inconvenient thoughts. His health of course became worse and worse by this hygiene, and he died young, of cancer. He came from Malmédy, near Aix-la-Chapelle, but lived in Paris from 1821. He was a great friend of Begas the painter."—*Trans.*

things in it, but mostly taken from Hummel's septett, on which the piece is really modelled. He played very well, though with some unsteadiness, on account of the fearful and unbearable heat. Just before he began he turned to Herz, and said with a sweet smile, 'Play for me, and I promise to give you ten sous.' But Herz, smilingly stroking his black beard, answered with a smile, 'Nay, that would not be agreeable to the public.' 'I beg your pardon,' said Kalkbrenner with another smile.

"Yesterday we were at the Feydeau, and saw the last act of an opera of Catel's, called 'L'Aubergiste,' and Auber's 'Léocadie.' The theatre is large, cheerful, and pretty; the orchestra very good; and if the fiddles are not as fine as those at the Opera Buffa, the basses and the wind and the *ensemble* are better; and the conductor stands in the middle. The singers do not sing badly, though they have no voices; their acting is lively and rapid, and the whole goes well together. But now for the chief thing, the composition. Of the first opera I will say nothing, for I only heard half of it, and that was poor and weak, though not without pretty, light melody; but the celebrated 'Léocadie,' by the celebrated Auber—anything so miserable you really cannot conceive. The story is taken from a wretched novel of Cervantes, wretchedly cooked up into an opera, and I could never have believed that so vulgar and objectionable a piece should not only hold its ground, but in a short time run through fifty-two representations before an audience of Frenchmen, who really have nice feeling and correct taste. To this novel, which belongs to Cervantes' wild period, Auber has made the most miserably tame music. I don't speak of there being no breadth, no life, no originality in the whole opera, and of its being patched together of alternate reminiscences of Cherubini and Rossini; I don't speak of there being no vestige of seriousness or spark of passion, no power, no fire in it, nor that in the greatest climaxes the singers have to make *roulades* and shakes and passages; but surely the favourite of the public, the pupil of Cherubini, a man with grey hair, might have been expected to know something about instrumentation, now that it has become so easy through the publication of the scores of Haydn, Mozart, and Beethoven! Not even that. Just fancy that out of the many pieces in the whole opera, there are perhaps three in which the piccolo does not play the chief part. The Overture begins with a *tremolando* in the strings, but very soon out pop the piccolo from the garret, and the bassoon from the cellar, and pipe away a melody between them. In the subject of the Allegro the strings have the Spanish accompaniment, and the piccolo tootles another air to it. Léocadie's first melancholy air, 'Pauvre Léocadie, il vaudrait mieux mourir,' is appropriately accompanied by a piccolo; the piccolo expresses the brother's rage, the lover's grief, the peasant girl's joy—in short, the whole thing might be capitally arranged for two flutes and a jew's-harp *ad libitum.* Oh dear!

"You tell me also, Fanny, that I ought to set up for a reformer, and teach people to like Onslow, Reicha, Beethoven, and Sebastian Bach. I do that already, as far as I can. But recollect, my dear child, that the people here don't know a note of 'Fidelio,' and look upon Bach as a mere full-bottomed wig, powdered with nothing but learning.

"The other day, at Kalkbrenner's request, I played Bach's organ preludes in E minor and A minor. The people thought them both sweetly pretty, and somebody remarked that the beginning of the A minor prelude bore a striking resemblance to a favourite duett of Monsigny's (a French opera writer)!——everything danced before my eyes.

"At Madame Kiené's a few days ago I played

my B minor quartett with Baillot. He began quite in a careless, indifferent sort of way, but at a passage in the first part of the first movement he got into the spirit of the thing, and played the rest of the movement and the Adagio very well and with plenty of vigour. Then came the Scherzo: I suppose the opening of it pleased him, for he went off like anything, at a tremendous pace, the others after him, I trying to keep them back; but it's not much good trying to keep back three runaway Frenchmen. And so they carried me along with them, always madder and madder and faster and louder; and especially at one place near the end, where the subject of the Trio comes at the top, against the beat, Baillot lashed away in the most furious style, in a rage with himself because he had made the same mistake several times over. When it was finished, all that he said to me was, 'Encore une fois ce morceau.' That time it went smoothly, but still more madly than the first time. The last movement at first went like wildfire. At that part near the end where the subject comes in for the last time in B minor, quite *fortissimo*, . Baillot sawed away at his strings in a perfect frenzy, so that I was almost frightened at my own quartett; and at the end, he came up to me, again without a word, and embraced me twice as if he wanted to stifle me. Rode also was very much pleased, and a long while afterwards, suddenly said to me in German: 'Bravo, mein Schatz!' . . . . Fanny,' you write to me of prejudices and partiality, of growling and owlishness, and of the land flowing with milk and honey—as you call this Paris. Just reflect, I beseech you, are you in Paris, or am I? Surely I must know more about it than you. Is it my way to let myself be hampered by prejudices in my judgment of music? And even if it were, is Rode prejudiced when he says, 'C'est une dégringolade musicale?' Is Neukomm prejudiced when he says, 'C'est pas ici le pays des orchestres?' Is Herz prejudiced when he says,

'The public here can understand and appreciate nothing but variations'? and are thousands of others prejudiced when they swear at Paris? It is you who are so prejudiced that you believe my impartial statements less than the lovely picture of an Eldorado Paris that your own fancy has drawn. Take up the *Constitutionnel*, what are they giving at the Italian opera besides Rossini? Take up a music-catalogue, what is published or sold but romances and potpourris? Wait till you have been here and heard 'Alceste,' 'Robin de Bois,' and the soirées; or till you have heard the music in the King's Chapel, and then judge and scold, but not now when you are hampered and regularly blinded by prejudices. But forgive me for this *Allegro feroce*.

"I have been busy these last days making a Kyrie *à* 5 *voce* and *grandissimo* orchestra: in bulk it surpasses anything I have yet written. There is also a tolerable amount of *pizzicato* in it, and as for the trombones, they will need good windpipes."*

This is a characteristic account of French musical life. It shows what a strictly artistic tendency the young musician had already developed at the early age of sixteen, and how unhesitatingly, in the very spirit of Goethe, he passed sentence on those who looked upon music as a mere trade.

Felix remained in Paris from the 23rd of March till the 19th of May; on the journey home he stopped at Weimar for a short visit, of which Goethe gives Zelter the following account:—
"Herr Mendelssohn stayed far too short a time on his way home. Felix produced his last new quartett, and astonished everyone with it. This personal and definite dedication through the ear pleased me very much. Felix told the ladies some things about the

---

* Letters to his parents of the 18th and 22nd April, 1825.

Parisian musical life, which were characteristic of the present time."

As an acknowledgment for the Dedication of the B minor quartett, Goethe soon after this sent his young friend what Zelter calls a "beautiful love-letter." It ran as follows :—

"You have given me very great pleasure, my dear Felix, by your valuable present; which, though already announced, took me by surprise. The print, the title-page, and the splendid binding, all vie with each other to make it a magnificent gift. I regard it as the graceful embodiment of that beautiful, rich, energetic soul which so astonished me when you first made me acquainted with it. Pray accept my very best thanks, and let me hope that you will soon give me another opportunity of admiring in person the fruits of your astonishing activity. Remember me to your good parents, your equally gifted sister, and your excellent master.

May a lively remembrance of me always be maintained in such a circle.

"Yours faithfully,

"J. W. GOETHE.

"WEIMAR, 18*th June*, 1825."

Goethe's kindly sympathy urged on the young artist to fresh and unceasing efforts. He completed his fifth * opera, and composed his Octett.† "He takes his time by the ears, and has his own way with it," writes Zelter. "A few weeks ago he gave his excellent tutor Heyse a most pleasant birthday present — namely, Terence's 'Andria' translated entirely by himself in metre; and it seems that there are some very good lines in it, but I have not yet seen it. He plays the piano like fury, and isn't backward at stringed instruments; and

---

* "Die Hochzeit des Camacho: Comic Opera in two Acts" (Op. 10).
† The well-known Octett for strings in E flat (Op. 20).

with all that he is strong and healthy, and can swim against the stream like anything.

"They have reviewed his quartetts and symphonies somewhat coldly in the musical paper, but it won't hurt him; for these reviewers are themselves but young fellows looking for the very hat they hold in their hands.

"If one did not remember how Gluck and Mozart were criticised forty years ago, one might lose heart. Things that are completely above the heads of these gentlemen, they cut up as coolly as possible, and fancy they can judge the whole house by one brick. And what I especially give him credit for, is the way in which he works at everything as a whole and with his whole might; and finishes whatever he begins, let it turn out as it will; and he therefore seldom shows any special affection for the finished things. Of course one now and then finds a little heterogeneous material, but it gets carried away by the stream, and ordinary faults and weaknesses are rare." *

"Now I must beg you," writes Goethe to Zelter after Felix had sent him his "Andria," "to be so good as to give my best thanks to the excellent and industrious Felix for this glorious specimen of his serious æsthetic studies; his work will be a special amusement for the circle of art-lovers at Weimar during the coming long winter evenings."

On the 20th February, 1827, Zelter continues his report as follows:—"My Felix has accepted an engagement at Stettin to perform his latest works there, and set off on the 16th. The dear boy attained his nineteenth year on the 3rd of this month, and his productions gain in ripeness and originality. His last opera, which occupies a whole evening, has been promised at the Theatre Royal for more than a year, but

* Letter of the 6th November, 1825.

has not yet managed to see the light; whereas all manner of French trash and rubbish gets put on the boards, and hardly survives a second representation. As we are young and able to stand against all the prejudices which embitter the best part of the lives of so many other people, it cannot do us much harm; but I do wish that with all his industry he may as quickly as possible grow out of this time of ours, for one has to be civil to it, whether one likes it or not; and in this I could still be of use to him, by making him lean more and more on himself."

In the summer of 1827, Felix matriculated at the Berlin University, and attended the lectures of Gans, Ritter, Lichtenstein, and Hegel. "Hegel," says Zelter, "is just giving a course of lectures on music; Felix writes them out thoroughly well, but, like a rogue, manages to introduce all Hegel's personal peculiarities in the most naïve manner.

"This Hegel says: 'There is no real music now; we have advanced, but we are not near the right thing by a long way.'—We know that as much or as little as he does, if he could only demonstrate to us musically whether he himself is on the right road. And so meanwhile we will go steadily onwards, *piano* and *sano*, as prompted by God whom we all serve. For we don't know what we ought to pray for, and always want more, and so others may do the same."

It was with the most lively interest that Goethe watched the process of development which Zelter describes in this original style. When he heard how Bach's gigantic "Passion" had been performed under the direction of Felix on the 11th March, 1829, after lying neglected for nearly a hundred years, he wrote to his friend: "It is just as if I heard the roaring of the sea from a distance. I wish you joy of so complete a success in that which is almost beyond achievement. I rejoice with all my heart in the satisfaction that Felix gives you: amongst my many pupils, I have not been so fortunate with more than a very few."

After Felix's accident during his journey in England in the summer of 1829, when he was thrown out of a carriage and hurt his knee, Goethe made many anxious inquiries after him in his letters to Zelter: "Above all, I want to know if there is favourable news of the good Felix. I feel the greatest interest in him, for it is most vexatious to see one who has turned out so remarkable, endangered by a tiresome accident, in the midst of progress and activity. Pray give me some consolation."

In the spring of 1830, when Felix had grown from a young man into a matured artist, he had again the satisfaction of beholding the face of the immortal master.

In Zelter's opinion the atmosphere of Berlin hindered and cramped the progress of his pupil.

He "feared," as he expressed himself, "to see him dissolve on the spot, like a jelly, in the midst of the pernicious and idle family tittle-tattle of the place. I can hardly await the time when the boy will be out of reach of all the confounded musical trash of Berlin, and get to Italy, where, to my mind, he ought to have gone long ago. There the very stones have ears, while here they eat lentils and pig's ears."

In his rough way the old Professor had hit the right nail on the head; for surely it is a blessing for any ardent nature to be able at the outset of life to shake off the restraint of home and see the world.

However hard the parting from their son might prove, his parents knew very well that the separation would be of real benefit to him, and it was determined that Felix should undertake a long journey. Before going to the birthplace of art, he was to seek the Poet's blessing on his visit to Rome "I have said nothing to my belongings," wrote Goethe when Zelter announced the approaching visit, "so that their delight at seeing Felix again may be heightened by the surprise;" and on the 21st of April, 1830, when the expected visitor was detained by an attack of measles, he asks: "How is it about Felix? Has he recovered, and are we soon to be rejoiced by his presence?"

When Felix arrived at Weimar in the end of May, he found Goethe outwardly unchanged, though at first somewhat silent and apathetic. "I think he wanted to see how I should take it; and I was vexed because I thought he had really become so. But luckily the conversation turned upon the Women's Societies of Weimar, and the 'Chaos,' an extravagant paper which the ladies publish among themselves, and to which I have ventured to become a contributor; and then old Goethe suddenly began to get jovial, and to chaff the two ladies about charitable doings, and would-be intellectualism and subscriptions, and sick-nursing, which he seems particularly to detest; he called me to join in the attack, and as I didn't wait to be asked twice he soon became quite his old self, and even more kind and confidential than he used to be with me. He stormed away at the universal sentimentality and melancholy of young men, reviled the exhibitions, and sales of work for the distressed, where the Weimar ladies had stalls, and nothing could be got because the young men settled it all beforehand amongst themselves, and the things were hidden till the right buyers came. After dinner, all at once he began 'Gute Kinder—hübsche Kinder, muss immer lustig sein — tolles Volk,' making eyes all the time like an old lion when he wants to go to sleep. Then I had to play to him, and he observed how strange it was that he had heard no music for so long a time, and meanwhile we had always been advancing, while he knew nothing of it; and so I ought to tell him a great deal about it all, for 'we must once more have a sensible talk together.' . . .

"As I had asked Goethe to call me 'Du,' he sent me word by Ottilie that in that case I must stay more than two days, or else he could not get into the way of it again. And then he repeated the same thing to me himself, and said I shouldn't miss anything if I stayed a little longer, and invited me to come to dinner every day, unless I wanted to go anywhere else; and as I have now been there every day, and yesterday had to tell him all about Scotland, and Hengstenberg, and Spontini, and Hegel's Æsthetics,—and as he sent me to Tiefurth with the ladies, forbidding me, however, to go on to Berka, because there was a beautiful girl living there, and he did not wish to plunge me into misery,—and as I felt that this was the very Goethe of whom people will one day declare that he is not at all *one* person, but is made up of several smaller Goethes——I should have been very foolish indeed if I had grudged the time."

And so the old merry life which they had led in the autumn of 1821 was begun again; they made music, and wrote doggrel rhymes, and when the old gentleman had gone to his room at nine o'clock, they danced, and never thought of separating before midnight.

Goethe commissioned a painter to make a portrait of the young artist for a collection of his friends' likenesses which he had for some time been making. Every morning he had a music lesson. This consisted in Felix's playing to him for an hour, pieces by all the great composers in chronological order, and then explaining what each had done to further the art. All the while he would sit in a dark corner, "like a Jupiter Tonans, with his old eyes flashing fire." At first he would not venture upon Beethoven at all. But when Felix declared he could not help it, and played the first movement of the C minor Symphony, he remarked, "That causes no emotion; it is only astonishing and grandiose;" and then, again, after muttering away to himself, he observed, "That is very grand, quite wild, enough to bring the house about one's ears; and what must it be when all the people are playing at once!"

After dinner he would remain alone in the room with his young friend for an hour, talking uninterruptedly. He brought out engravings and explained them, and talked about "Hernani" and Lamartine's Elegies, and the theatre, and pretty girls; and although he generally saw but little company, he now again invited people to come and hear Felix play, and openly expressed his admiration before them with his favourite word, "Ganz stupend!" Then he got together the beauties of Weimar, and exhorted him to pay court to them: "My dear fellow, you must go to the women and make yourself very sweet to them." When Ottilie asked whether Felix did not come too often, he grumbled out: "Why, I am only just beginning to have proper talks with him, and he is so clear-headed about his own subjects, that I must learn a great deal from him." He would not hear of his departure, and drew Ottilie aside from the company to a window to say to her, "You must manage to make him stay;" and when her persuasions had failed, he came out into the garden himself to add his own, and to assure Felix that there was no hurry for him to go, that he had much more to tell him, and in return wanted to hear a great deal more music; that Weimar was really the aim of his young friend's journey, and that it was impossible to imagine what he could wish for here that he would find at the *tables d'hôte*. Ottilie and Ulrike helped, and reminded him how the old gentleman never pressed people to stay, but so much oftener obliged them to go, and how it fell to nobody's lot to have their share of happy days so fixed that they might throw away the certainty of any; . . . adding that they would accompany him to Jena. Who could have resisted such representations? Felix remained, and had every reason not to repent of his decision; he speaks of the following day, the 1st of June, as the most delightful which he had ever spent there; he tells how, after driving through the park, he found the old gentleman in the best of humours, and how he began talking, and got into one of those conversations which one never forgets all one's life. Goethe set out with rallying his young friend about his various passions, great and small, for the beauties of Weimar. "Jenny von Pappenheim," he said,* "is as beautiful, as unconsciously graceful and charming, as a piece of phosphorescent wood or a glow-worm by daylight, which one can't

---

* The following is from my father's unpublished diary.

see." Two other girls, the Spiegels, "gave one the feeling of looking at a couple of great rose-bushes. . . . . I had a monstrous one in my garden which blossomed magnificently, but when these girls stood in front of it, one could see nothing but them." . . . . Then he got to talking about the "Muette de Portici," the Englishman Stendhal,* and Walter Scott. "Mr. Stendhal is one of the mediocre sort; he is intelligent and has a certain amount of knowledge, but the best and highest he has not got. 'Waverley' is Scott's best novel, and contains all

---

* Stendhal was a Frenchman, whose real name was Marie-Henri Beyle, that of Stendhal being adopted as a *nom de plume*. He was born at Grenoble in 1783, subsequently became attached to the household of Napoleon I., and followed the French army in the campaigns of 1812–14. After 1814 he resided at Milan, and devoted himself to literature. His chief writings are biographies of Haydn and Mozart (which he translated literally from the "Haydine" of Carpani, and published without acknowledgment under the name of Bombet), of Metastasio and Rossini; a History of Painting in Italy, essays, romances, &c. His writings display great originality and a superior mind, though his inaccuracies are frequent, and his opinions often startling.—*Trans.*

his succeeding works; without being brilliant, it is sufficiently interesting;—so is 'The Fair Maid of Perth.' It is amusing to see how Scott always styles himself the 'Author of Waverley.' Iffland began just in the same way with his 'Jägern,' which contains all his good and bad points; and so did Kotzebue with his 'Menschenhass und Reue,' which to this day makes all the women cry their eyes out, though a man would only scratch his head over it."

"Schiller," observed Felix, "at any rate did not begin in that manner."

"Schiller," continued Goethe, "was obliged to make a complete change after 'Don Carlos,' he could not have gone on in that style; though even at the present day people are fond of seeing 'The Robbers,' because many of them are still in that same insane and ridiculous state of mind. When I was director of the theatre at Lauchstedt, the students begged me to give 'The

Robbers,' but I declined for fear of a disturbance; however, as they promised me on their honour to keep quiet, I said: 'You are delightful, charming people, and if you will be very orderly you shall have it.' The house was immensely full, the public quiet as mice, even 'Ein freies Leben' was sung with the greatest gravity; and as they had behaved so well, and had also brought in some money, I was able the next day to praise them.

"Schiller understood what I never could do —namely, how to introduce matters of fact into his works; while he was writing 'Tell,' he read Swiss history, and had maps and drawings and the like hanging up in his room. There was something terrific in his progress; if you had not seen him for a week, you found him quite changed, and did not know what to make of him for astonishment. He went forward unceasingly till his forty-sixth year, and then came the end. He could have produced two tragedies every year; but not more, excepting translations and contributions to the *Musen-Almanach*, and so forth. A hundred *carolins* are not to be despised, and he needed them for himself and his wife. He had asked the Duke for a moderate salary, on the agreement that it should be doubled as soon as he was unfit for work; and the Duke gave it very willingly, for he was rather covetous of great men, and in such matters did more in Weimar than any king."

"He was rewarded for it," observed Felix.

"Yes," said Goethe, "he cannot be removed from the place which he now occupies in the world's history. He wanted to secure Schuckmann, and I corresponded with him about it; and Schlosser also, but I dissuaded him from that, because Schlosser was too unbending and immovable on his standpoint, as well as somewhat pedantic; he was my brother-in-law, so you see I did not show much tendency to nepotism.

And so this place became a sort of general focus. Oh if I could but write a fourth volume of my life! but there's no getting at it, what with botany, and meteorology, and all the other foolish things that no one will ever thank me for. It would be such a history of the year 1775, as nobody could know or write as I could. How at that time the nobility began to feel itself rather eclipsed by the middle class, and had to make exertions so as not to be left behind; how Liberalism, Jacobinism, and all other inventions of the evil one cropped up; how one began a new life here, working and producing, and occasionally at the right moment falling in love, and thereby disturbing one's peace of mind; and how the aristocratical spirit of Nicolai and the other Berliners, which was thought a good deal of at that time, had to be taken down by us young men—for, in spite of all our awkwardness, we had plenty of spirit and energy; then there was Schiller's first visit to

Weimar, when he left it without being noticed by anyone; and then came Jean Paul, but found the circle already closed; and after him Bertuch, who was bent upon being practical, and tried to produce everything that could possibly be wanted, and ended by founding the '*Industrie-komptoir*'! Yes, that time was like the spring, when everything is bursting into life, and one tree stands bare, while another is already in full leaf. So it was in 1775!"

The young artist listened with the liveliest interest to the ardent words in which the old Poet thus recalled his youth and the intellectual spring of 1775. "It was one of those conversations which one can never forget, all one's life." He showed plainly how touched and delighted he was, and when he thanked Goethe, the latter answered: "Well, it's a mere chance; it all came out quite incidentally, called forth by the charm of your presence." Then he asked for several of his favourite Mozart pieces, the C minor Fantasia, a Haydn Trio, and a Weber Capriccio, and promised his young friend "something important" as a parting gift. The next day he gave him a sheet of the autograph of "Faust" inscribed with the following words: "To my dear young friend F. M. B., the powerful and gentle ruler of the piano, as a remembrance of happy May days in 1830. J. W. v. GOETHE."

Felix had mentioned a picture of Ostade's representing a peasant family at prayer, which had made a great impression on him in 1821; and when he came into the Poet's room on the morning of the 3rd of June to take leave, he found Goethe sitting before a large portfolio looking at this very picture. "Yes, yes," said the old Poet in a solemn tone, "the hour has come, and we must see that we keep straight till your return; but we must not part from one another without a moment's devotion, and so let us look at this 'Prayer' together for a little while." "Then he told me that I was to write to him sometimes—("Courage! courage! I shall do it from here," writes Felix home)—and then he kissed me, and we drove off to Jena."

Goethe, in a letter to Zelter, gives his own impression of the visit as follows: "Just now, at half-past nine, with the clearest sky and the brightest sunshine, the excellent Felix, having spent a fortnight with us very pleasantly, and enchanted everybody by the perfection and charm of his art, is driving off with Ottilie, Ulrike, and the children, to Jena, there also to delight his friends, and leaves behind him a memory which deserves to be for ever cherished.

"His coming did me a great deal of good, for my feelings about music are unchanged; I hear it with pleasure, interest and reflection; I love its history, for who can understand any subject without thoroughly initiating himself into its origin and progress? It is a great thing that Felix fully recognizes the value of going through its successive stages, and happily his memory is so good as to furnish him with any number of examples of all kinds. From the Bach period downwards, he has brought Haydn, Mozart, and Gluck to life for me, has given me clear ideas of the great modern masters of *technique*, and lastly has made me understand his own productions, and given me plenty to think about in himself. He took away with him my warmest blessing."

Goethe sent another earnest request to his departing guest, through Ottilie, that he would write often, and thus "revive his charming presence" amongst them.

In a letter from Ottilie of the 8th June, we read as follows: "We feel like people who don't know how to fill up a blank; or like schoolboys, who find everything excessively dull after the holidays: in these descriptions I include my papa. You see, dear Felix, what an advantage you have over us? If you feel a reaction and are tempted to grumble, I am sure you only do it in the most touching sounds, whilst ours buzz round our heads like bats, and don't exactly make us pleasanter. My father sends you word that your stay here, besides giving him great pleasure, was of lasting use to him, as you have made him understand so many things."

At Munich Felix mustered courage to write to Goethe himself, thanking him for the ever memorable days which he had enjoyed, and describing the life in Munich, and the artists to whom the Poet had given him introductions: "Stieler in particular was wonderfully kind and amiable to me. The way in which he spoke of you and yours, the beaming delight which overspread his whole person when he recalled the time he had spent with you, made me at once feel specially drawn towards him. He is painting your 'Fisher,' and told me that the picture originated partly in his dislike to one which had made a great sensation at the Berlin Exhibition, and in which the subject was treated in far too sensuous a manner. It may be true, but I don't know how he is to succeed in entirely avoiding the difficulty, for if you are to have the figure of a woman rising fresh from the water, and at the same time singing and speaking in a lovely way, she must be charming, and the Fisherman to whom she beckons must be a beautiful graceful youth; whereas his picture seems to me to be based on quite another idea. But as yet it is only sketched-in, and at any rate the head of the nymph is already so graceful and pretty that she is sure to give universal pleasure. Stieler has also just finished a portrait for the King's private collection of beauties, and is perpetually looking about amongst the Munich girls for new models. He is delighted with this commission, and no wonder, for the ladies pay him no end of attention, and would give anything to please him so that he may give them the prize, and pick them out as the most beautiful.

"Music is very much run after here, and there is plenty of it, but it seems to me that almost everything makes an impression in this place, and that the impression does not last. It is most amusing to see the difference between a Munich and a Berlin musical party. At Berlin, when a piece of music comes to an end, the whole company sits in solemn silence, each one considering what his opinion is to be, nobody giving a sign of applause or pleasure, and all the while the performer is in the most painful embarrassment, not knowing whether, and in what spirit, he has been listened to. And yet, afterwards, he often finds people who have given all their attention, and been very deeply moved, though outwardly appearing so cold and indifferent. Here, on the contrary, it is great fun playing at a party, because the people can't help talking every minute about what they like; sometimes even they begin clapping and applauding in the middle of a piece; and it is not at all uncommon, when one gets up from playing, to find that everybody has moved, because sometimes all of a sudden they want to come and watch one's fingers, and stand all round the piano, or some one wishes to make an observation to some one else, and goes and sits down by him and talks. Afterwards they overwhelm you with compliments and kindness; but I don't know whether I should not be afraid that, after a day or two, much of the vividness of the impression would fade.*

* This contrast between North and South Germany also struck Schumann. He says in one of his papers (*Gesammelte Schriften*, iii. 233), àpropos to Liszt's reception at Dresden, " do not know the applause-thermometer of the Dresden public well enough to

"The Opera is supplied in the amplest manner, and yet does not produce anything out of the common way, because there is no leading spirit to direct the whole thing. Schechner, for example, is one of the most remarkable singers we have; but because they praise her good points up to the skies, and pass over her failings, she is accustoming herself, by degrees, to all sorts of mannerisms. It seems moreover to be thought *bon ton* to abuse the opera and the theatre, and to pay much attention to the critics, who try to earn their scanty daily bread by scoffing and sneering; this again discourages the actors, the bitterness increases on both sides, and thus it arises that there is seldom much pleasure or real enjoyment to be had at the theatre."

Felix's second letter to Goethe is dated " Rome,

judge of the impression he produced. Of all Germans the Viennese spare their hands least, and in their idolatry have been known to clap till they split their gloves—but in North Germany it is different."

March the 5th, 1831," and gives a lively and amusing sketch of artistic life in the Eternal City. "A few German artists are to be seen with long hair and moustaches, turned down collars, old-fashioned German coats, tobacco-pipes, and bull-dogs. It does not seem as if the great masters, or the desire to learn, had anything to do with their coming here. In their opinion Raphael is weak, and Titian merely a good colourist."

"Niebuhr," remarked Goethe, when telling Eckermann[*] about this letter from Felix, "was right when he predicted a time of barbarism; it is here already, we are in the midst of it, for in what else does barbarism consist but in not recognizing what is really good?"

Felix's description of the Carnival, the election of the new Pope, the Revolution that broke out immediately afterwards, the courageous behaviour of Horace Vernet, and the pitiable cowardice of

[*] Conversation of March 22nd, 1831.

the German painters, gave the Poet occasion to speak of the "mental perversion which originating forty years before in a few individuals had now pervaded the German artists. Their doctrine was, that the main things necessary to enable an artist to equal the greatest, were piety and genius. Such a doctrine was very insinuating, and was eagerly caught at; for no learning is necessary to make one pious, and genius everybody inherits from his mother. It is sufficient to utter something which flatters self-conceit and indolence, for it to be sure of a favourable reception with the public."

By this "mental infection" Felix was in no danger of being attacked.

"Before I say anything else," writes Goethe to Zelter, "I must tell you that I have got a most charming and detailed letter from Felix, dated Rome, March the 5th, giving a delightful account of the excellent fellow. He will no doubt give the same, in an equally modest spirit, to his parents and his Berlin friends.* It is not necessary to be anxious about him any longer; his talents, like a beautiful swimming-belt, will bear him safely even through the waves and breakers of this alarming barbarism."

Thus did Goethe's warm sympathy accompany his young friend on his wanderings. The Poet was quite angry with his father for not allowing him, after all his ready compliance, to extend his journey to Sicily, as he wished to do. "Italy without Sicily does not leave a complete image on the mind. It is a very great mistake of the Herr Papa not to send our good Felix to Sicily, for now he will come away with an unsatisfied longing."

Felix had long cherished the idea of composing Goethe's "Walpurgisnacht;" on leaving Vienna he had begun to work at it, and

* See the letters of March 8th, 15th, &c. in the "Reisebriefe."

managed to finish it during his Italian journey, in spite of the difficulty of the subject. Goethe expressed his approbation and pleasure on hearing that his young friend had undertaken what Zelter had attempted in vain, and in the following words sketched out for him the fundamental ideas of the poem:—" The principles on which this poem is based are symbolic in the highest sense of the word. For in the history of the world, it must continually recur that an ancient, tried, established, and tranquillizing order of things will be forced aside, displaced, thwarted, and, if not annihilated, at least pent up within the narrowest possible limits by rising innovations. The intermediate period, when the opposition of hatred is still possible and practicable, is forcibly represented in this poem, and the flames of a joyful and undisturbed enthusiasm once more blaze high in brilliant light."

During his return from Italy Felix gave a more lengthened and detailed description of his travels in Switzerland. Writing to Goethe from Lucerne on the 28th of August, 1831, he says :* "I could not leave out Switzerland, which has always been my favourite country. I shall never forget this time that I have spent roaming about the mountains on foot, all alone, without knowing a creature, and thinking of nothing but the new and wonderfully beautiful things that burst upon me every moment.

"I came from the land of bright skies and warmth; but Switzerland gave me a very different reception: I found rain and storms and mist, and on the mountains often had to go through snowstorms. But somehow or other, I rather liked it; and occasionally, when the great black rocky peaks emerge from the clouds, or a whole

* Through the kindness of Professor Mendelssohn, I am enabled to insert the whole of this letter, of which in the original he has only given portions. The autograph appears to have suffered much bad usage; it contains at present neither signature, address, nor date, and it was only by a minute and careful comparison that its date could be fixed with certainty.—*Translator.*

reach of country seems to burst into sunshine out of the midst of the fog, it is quite glorious. No amount of bad weather could stop me from climbing about as much as possible; sometimes the guide refused to go with me, often I could not see anything at all, but still I did what I could, and when a fine day came at last, it was a double pleasure. Here, Nature seems to make even a grander impression on me than elsewhere, for I am more completely surrounded by her, and the whole country and people depend entirely and solely upon her.

"You must have heard of the terrible inundations and storms in the Bernese Oberland; I was there just at the time, and it was awful to see how everything connected with human beings, even the most durable things,—streets, bridges, meadows and houses,—could so easily disappear in a moment, without leaving a trace —as if they had never existed. Three days afterwards Nature was all calm and smiling again, as if nothing had happened, and the people at work to restore order as far as possible. I was just then on my way to the lake of Thun, without a guide, and quite alone. Since that day when you told me about your observations on the weather and on clouds, I have taken a special interest in the subject, and paid more attention to what was going on above me. I could distinctly see the gradual way in which the storm came on; the clouds had been gathering for two days, and at last, on the evening of the 7th, a great thunderstorm burst forth, and went on the whole night, with continual rain. In the morning it looked as if clouds were coming down instead of rain. I never saw clouds lie so low before; they had stationed themselves all about round the bases of the mountains, far down into the valleys, quite thick and white, with overhead nothing but black mist. It did not rain at all for a little while, till the lower clouds began to float up and down, and then the rain went on again for that whole day and the following night; but the actual masses of clouds and mist only collected on the third morning, the 9th, and then the whole breadth of the horizon and the sky was completely filled with them. Storms generally come up with a clear sky; but in this case the masses of clouds piled themselves one upon another, and were driven across country from the plains in the north-west, right into the mountains on the south-east. It was impossible to distinguish the opposite side of the lake. In the intervals, when one layer of clouds had passed, it stopped raining, but in another minute it began pouring down out of the next one with indescribable fury. The footpaths were soon under water, streams were running across the roads in every direction, and the mountain-torrents came rushing down like mad, quite dark-brown, so that they looked like mere dark earth boiling up out of the river-bed, and being dashed into the lake; —you could see the dark streams far out upon the clear water. The smaller bridges had already been all carried off in the morning, the piers and arches of the large stone ones were also torn away, and one forest-stream brought a lot of furniture and household goods into the lake with it, without anybody's knowing what houses had been demolished. Some days afterwards, when the rain had ceased, and I came into the valley of Lauterbrunnen, the broad high road had completely vanished, and the ground where it had been was nothing but a heap of shingle and sand and great blocks of stone, for fully a mile. The same damage had been done on that day almost all over the country, on the St. Gothard, at Unterwalden, Glarus, &c. Sometimes it was difficult to get along, and one had to go over the mountains, because the water left no room in the valleys,—but that only made it all the finer on the mountains.

"I spent last week at Engelberg, in an Unterwald monastery several thousand feet above the sea, perfectly secluded, where I found a nice organ and pleasant monks. They had never heard of Sebastian Bach, so that a few of his fugues on the organ were a complete novelty to them; but still they were pleased, and on the saint's day (St. Bartholomew's) I had to play the organ for them, accompany the Mass, and make the Responses. It was the first time on this journey that I had got hold of a decent organ, for in Italy I didn't find a single one in good order. Besides this, the monks had a nice library; and as neither politics, strangers, nor newspapers ever enter the valley, I had a pleasant time of it there.

"At last the weather cleared up again, and to-day it is as if Nature herself wanted to celebrate this great occasion.* The sky is of the brightest blue, the mountains have decked themselves in their most brilliant colours, the landscape looks gay and festal,—all seem to know what an important day it is.

"I have just come from the theatre,—the only one in all Switzerland,—and have been hearing Schiller's 'William Tell.' This being the time of the Diet, the Swiss depart from their custom of preferring no theatre to a bad one. And as it is the only one in the country, you must allow me to say a few words about so national a performance. The whole troupe numbers about ten persons, and the stage is the size and height of a small room; but still they wanted to give the crowded scenes. So two men in pointed hats represented Gessler's army, two others in round hats the Swiss country people, and the subordinate parts were done away with.

* Goethe's last birthday.

Whenever there was anything important to say, they left it out without compunction, and coolly went on with the next words in their parts without any connection, and occasionally with the most comic effect. Some of the actors had only learnt the drift of their parts, and made their own verses on the spot; Gessler's envoy, with the first beat, knocked the drum out of his button-hole on to the ground, and could not fasten it on again, to the great delight of the liberty-loving public, who laughed heartily at the tyrant's slave; but it was impossible to kill the piece entirely, and even with all this it was effective. When the familiar names and places occurred, which one had seen the day before, the people were in raptures, nudging one another and pointing to the pasteboard lake, which they could see far better in the reality by walking out of their houses.

"But it was Gessler who gave the greatest

delight, because he behaved so uproariously, and ranted and raged in such furious style; his dishevelled beard, red nose, and cap all awry, made him look just like a drunken workman; the whole thing was quite Arcadian and primitive, like the infancy of the drama."

Before this, in the Engelberg valley, Felix had been regaling himself with reading "Tell," and had called to mind Goethe's remark that "Schiller could have *produced* two such tragedies every year." "This craftsmanlike expression suddenly struck me very forcibly when reading the play in all its freshness and life, and such activity appeared to me so prodigiously grand that it made me feel as if I had never yet done anything properly all my life. Everything of mine is so fragmentary, and I feel as if I too must some day produce something."

The performance at Lucerne must have recalled afresh the same remarkable conversation about Schiller. It is well known what a strong attraction the story had for Goethe, and how, in 1797, when excited by that incomparable landscape, he seriously occupied himself with the idea of writing an epic poem on "Tell," though he subsequently abandoned the subject to his friend. "I already hummed over my hexameters at leisure moments.* The subject engrossed me so completely that I could see the lake in the calm moonlight, with the mists lighting up the hollows of the mountains, as well as in the loveliest morning sunlight, with the woods and meadows breaking out into jubilant life. Then I brought in a thunder-storm, sweeping out of the ravines upon the lake. Nor was there any lack of nightly stillness, or of secret meetings by bridge and glen."

And with this glorious landscape as a background, what a contrast do Goethe's characters present to Schiller's!—his Tell, a porter wandering through the canton, a self-satisfied, childish

* Conversation with Eckermann, May 6th, 1827.

unconscious hero: his Gessler, a tyrant of the comfortable order, who "does a good action now and then, by way of a joke;" and by the side of these more passive figures the real characters of the liberators, the Fürsts, Stauffachers, and Winkelrieds!

The contrast between the two greatest German poets is seen in the characteristic variety of their treatment of the same material. Goethe afterwards toned down, or omitted, several forcible traits which Schiller had wished to introduce. "I know well the difficulty I had with him about 'Tell,' when he wanted to make Gessler pick an apple straight from the tree, and shoot it off the boy's head. This was quite against my principles, and I persuaded him at least to suggest some motive for such cruelty, by making Tell's son boast that his father was so good a marksman that he could strike an apple from a tree at a hundred paces. Schiller did not at first take to the idea, though finally he yielded to my representations and entreaties, and did what I advised."

Though it was with real pleasure, and no envious feelings, that Goethe watched the labours of his literary friend, he was clearly conscious how entirely opposite were his own sentiments. How telling, for example, is his remark to Felix in reference to Schiller's "terrific progress," and that it was "impossible for him to sustain it beyond his forty-sixth year"! To Eckermann he further* expressed himself to the effect that in his youth Schiller was too much influenced by physical freedom, and that in maturer life, when he had had enough of physical freedom, he drifted into ideal freedom. "And I might almost say that this idea killed him. For it caused him to make demands on his physical nature which were too much for his powers. . . . He used to force himself to work for days and

* Conversation of 18th January, 1827.

weeks when he was not well, with the view of making his powers obey him, and be at his command at all times. . . .

"All those passages in his writings, which some wiseacres declare to be inconsistent, I would call 'pathological' passages, because they were written on days when he had not the power to discover his real, true motives. I have all possible respect for the 'categorical imperative,' and know how much good may proceed from it; but one must not push it too far, for then the idea of ideal freedom can lead to no good." In these warnings against the exaggeration of the "categorical imperative," and this verdict on his friend, so restlessly indefatigable, so early snatched away, we see the perfect and healthy realism of Goethe's nature.

To Felix, these words of Goethe's supplied a fresh spur to increased activity: "There is an enormous deal to do in the world," he writes, "and I will be industrious. To-day I understand for the first time what deep meaning there is in Goethe's words about Schiller, and feel that I must bestir myself."

From Switzerland he travelled by way of Munich to Paris, where he renewed the impressions of the summer of 1825. "The political life there," writes Zelter to Goethe, "no less than the artistic, seems only to strengthen Felix's love for his own country."

It was in Paris that Felix received the news of the death[*] of the poet who had shown him the ideal of German Art. "How poor one feels after such a loss as Goethe's!" he writes to his parents on the 31st of March. "How it changes the aspect of the whole country! It is a piece of news that will always be brought back to me by the name of Paris, and the impression of it is one which no kindness, nor any of the bustle and excitement of the gay life here, can ever efface."

[*] March 22, 1832.

All great minds shared the depression of the young artist, who had enjoyed the advantage of Goethe's society.

Zelter, drawn by a mysterious and mighty longing, followed his friend to the grave a few weeks later. With Goethe no longer there to look up to, the world seemed desolate and empty. All missed the peaceful harmony, and the genial brightness, which had kept every antagonism within bounds, and had shed a light on life.

APPENDIX.

APPENDIX.

The following letters have not yet been published in any permanent shape; and though not immediately connected with the period of Mendelssohn's life which forms the subject of the previous portion of this volume, they cannot fail to be valuable to all who take an interest in his character and his career.

(1.) *To* Herr Gustav Preusser, *Leipzig.**

(Translation.)

London, 29*th June*, 1842.

My dear Herr Preusser,

Yesterday I received from my brother in Berlin the good news that I need not be there in the beginning of August, so that on our side there is nothing to interfere with the charming plans for the summer.

* From the original in the possession of Madame Preusser.

How will it be about the Swiss journey? I might really end my letter here, and wait impatiently for your answer, for everything else is contained in that question. How splendid it would be, and what a delight it would be for us, if our lovely plan could really be crowned in this most lovely way. But all this we have already talked over, and you know it, and why should I repeat it? If you can possibly manage it, I do hope you will not deny us, and I may add yourself too, this pleasure. And even if you had to make sacrifices for it yourself, I should like to worry you into it, provided only it lies within the limits of possibility; for such a journey is a lasting and ever new pleasure for one's whole lifetime, and you may perhaps never again have such a summer for it, or such glorious bright weather. To be sure you might find pleasanter travelling companions, but certainly none who would be so glad to have you, and to whom you could give greater pleasure by your presence; and I can promise you that we should get on splendidly together. Our present idea is to leave Frankfort towards the end of July, and spend August in Switzerland. Of course we would gladly change our plans if it should not suit you. Only you must be quick, and tell me what you think about it. I should like best if you merely wrote "Yes!" addressed to Frankfort, to the Souchay's house, at the "Fahrthor." What a treat, what a joy that would be for us!

My wife will add a few words to your letter; I find it more difficult than ever to write letters from here, for we lead such a curious and exciting life, and the English are so mad about me this time (I mean they are so kind), that I often come home in the evening quite giddy, and don't know where my head is. But we will talk about all this, please God, on some meadow or beautiful mountain. And now give my love to the whole dear, kind family, and especially to my two very dear nieces (the whole letter is addressed to your wife as well), and to Caroline, and Louise, and quite particularly to my darling godchild, and, in fact, to the whole house (including the front door, and the bell that I know so intimately); and give Schleinitz and David a hundred thousand remembrances from me, and tell them that I often long to see them, and that they might have written to me once, and so might I to them,—and pray forgive these hasty lines. And think it over, and if it lies within the limits of possibility come with us for a lovely trip into that lovely country.

Ever yours, fondly and faithfully,
FELIX MENDELSSOHN BARTHOLDY.

(2.) *To his Mother.**

(Translation.)

FRANKFORT, *July* 19, 1842.

DEAR LITTLE MOTHER,

Here we are again, all well and happy, after a delightful journey. We found the dear children in the best health and spirits, and your dear letter reports the same of you all. One lovely day follows another and brings the same beautiful blue sky and warm balmy air. If only one knew how to be grateful enough for all such great pleasures! It is so sweet to be here in Frankfort again, in the midst of so many dear friends and relations, and such a lovely neighbourhood. Every morning at six I go for a walk towards the Darmstadt Observatory, and when I come back the children are just up, and all at breakfast, and then the thought of Paul and Albertine and Switzerland does not depress me so very much. If God would but fulfil all our pleasant prospects, and take our rejoicings for past and future ones as thanks! Cécile made up her mind this morning to go with me, and leave the children here with her mother, who enjoys having them above all things. I know that Cécile will repent

* From the original, published by Dr. Karl Mendelssohn in *Ueber Land und Meer* for 1871, No. 14.

of it often enough before it comes to the point; but
I hope I may be able to keep her up to the mark,
and the Pauls will do their part also.

Yesterday evening, just as I was driving to the Mühl-
derg with Veit and Bernus, we met Hiller and his
wife; on the steamer we travelled with Madame
Matthieu, then with Herr and Madame Rubens; at
Mainz we had a chat with the Woringens, who went
with us to the railway station (Prince Frederic—on
his way back from Rome—detained us so long on the
road that we very nearly came too late); then there
were Schlemmer and his wife fresh from Ems, Julie
Schunk-Jeanrenaud (much better) from Dresden, and
Rosenhain from Paris, Benecke senior from London,
Ditto junior from his property,—all meeting at the
gate; such is our life every day!

I must tell you a little more about London and
the days after our trip to Manchester. I could not
make up my mind to go to Dublin because of the
twelve hours' sea journey, the thought of which crushed
all my ideas. We spent two peaceful days in Manchester with the uncles and aunts, but as soon as we
got back to London the whirl began again. I shall
tell you all about it verbally—how disgracefully Cécile
carried on with Sir Edward Bulwer, and how old Rogers
(Sam Rogers, you know) squeezed her hand and begged

her to bring up her children to be as charming as herself, and to speak English as well (this made a sensation), and how Mr. Roebuck came in (ask Dirichlet who he is),—*à propos*, at Aix-la-Chapelle we paid the Meyers a proper visit, but at Cologne we could only stop twenty minutes, so were unable to look up Louise Hensel,—and how we played charades at the Beneckes', and Klingemann acted a West India planter and Sir Walter Scott, and how the Directors of the Philharmonic gave me a fish dinner at Greenwich with whitebait and speeches, and how they sung my Antigone music at the Moscheles' (I must imitate that on the piano for your benefit—I see Beckchen laughing already: but why does she never write?)—and how I waited for Herr von Massow at the Brunswick Hotel, and spoke to Herr Abeken at the Bunsens'—and how we had a great dinner at the Bunsens'—all this I shall describe minutely when I see you; but I must at once tell you all the details of my last visit at Buckingham Palace. I know how it will amuse you, dear mother, and me too.

It is, as Grahl says, the one really pleasant and thoroughly comfortable English house, where one feels *à son aise*. Of course I do know a few others, but yet on the whole I agree with him. Joking apart, Prince Albert had asked me to go to him on Saturday at two o'clock, so that I might try his organ before I left England; I found him alone, and as we were talking away the Queen came in, also alone, in a simple morning dress. She said she was obliged to leave for Claremont in an hour, and then suddenly interrupting herself exclaimed, "But goodness, what a confusion!" for the wind had littered the whole room, and even the pedals of the organ (which, by the way, made a very pretty feature in the room), with leaves of music from a large portfolio that lay open. As she spoke she knelt down and began picking up the music; Prince Albert helped, and I too was not idle. Then Prince Albert proceeded to explain the stops to me, and she said that she would meanwhile put things straight. I begged that the Prince would first play me something, so that, as I said, I might boast about it in Germany; and he played a Choral, by heart, with the pedals, so charmingly and clearly and correctly that it would have done credit to any professional, and the Queen, having finished her work, came and sat by him and listened and looked pleased. Then it was my turn, and I began my chorus from "St. Paul" —"How lovely are the messengers." Before I got to the end of the first verse they both joined in the chorus, and all the time Prince Albert managed the stops for me so cleverly—first a flute, at the forte the great organ, at the D major part the whole, then he made a lovely diminuendo with the stops, and so on to the end of the piece, and all by heart—that I was really quite enchanted. Then the young Prince of Gotha came in, and there was more chatting; and the Queen asked if I had written any new songs, and she said she was very fond of singing my published ones. "You should sing one to him," said Prince Albert; and after a little begging, she said she would try the "Frühlingslied"* in B flat—"if it is still here," she added, "for all my music is packed up for Claremont." Prince Albert went to look for it, but came back, saying it was already packed. "But one might perhaps unpack it," said I. "We must send for Lady ——," she said (I did not catch the name). So the bell was rung, and the servants were sent after it, but without success; and at last the Queen went herself, and while she was gone Prince Albert said to me, "She begs you will accept this present as a remembrance," and gave me a little case with a beautiful ring, on which is engraved "V. R. 1842." Then the Queen came back and said, "Lady —— is gone, and has taken all my things with her. It really is most annoying." (You can't think how that amused me.) I then begged that I might not be made to suffer for the accident,

* Op. 47, No. 3.

and hoped she would sing another song. After some consultation with her husband he said, "she will sing you something of Gluck's." Meantime the Princess of Gotha had come in, and we five proceeded through various corridors and rooms to the Queen's sitting-room, where there was a gigantic rocking-horse standing near the sofa, and two big bird-cages, and pictures on the walls, and splendidly bound books on the table, and music on the piano. The Duchess of Kent came in too, and while they were all talking I rummaged about amongst the music, and soon discovered my first set of songs. So, of course, I begged her rather to sing one of those than the Gluck, to which she very kindly consented; and which did she choose?— "Schöner und schöner schmückt sich!"* sung it quite charmingly in strict time and tune, and with very good execution. Only in the line "Der Prosa Lasten und Müh," where it goes down to D, and then comes up again so closely, she sang D sharp each time, and as I gave her the note the two first times, the last time she sang D, and there it ought to have been D sharp. But with the exception of this little mistake it was really charming, and the last long G I have never heard better, or purer, or more natural from any amateur. Then I was obliged to confess that Fanny

* "Italien"—Op. 8, No. 3.

had written the song (which I found very hard, but pride must have a fall), and beg her to sing one of my own also. If I would give her plenty of help she would gladly try, she said, and then she sang the Pilgerspruch,* "Lass dich nur," really quite faultlessly, and with charming feeling and expression. I thought to myself, one must not pay too many compliments on such an occasion, so I merely thanked her a great many times; upon which she said, "Oh, if only I had not been so frightened; generally I have such long breath." Then I praised her heartily and with the best conscience in the world; for just that part with the long C at the close she had done so well, taking it and the three notes next to it all in the same breath, as one seldom hears it done—and therefore it amused me doubly that she herself should have begun about it. After this Prince Albert sang the Aerndte-lied,† "Es ist ein Schnitter;" and then he said I must play him something before I went, and gave me as themes the Choral which he had played on the organ and the song he had just sung. If everything had gone as usual, I ought to have improvised dreadfully badly, for it is almost always so with me when I want it to go well, and then I should have gone away vexed with the whole morn-

* Op. 8, No. 5.   † Op. 8, No. 4.

ing. But, just as if I were to keep nothing but the pleasantest, most charming recollection of it, I never improvised better; I was in the best mood for it and played a long time, and enjoyed it myself so that besides the two themes I brought in the song that the Queen had sung, naturally enough; and it all went off so easily that I would gladly not have stopped; and they followed me with so much intelligence and attention that I felt more at my ease than I ever did in improvising to an audience. She said several times she hoped I would soon come to England again and pay them a visit, and then I took leave, and down below I saw the beautiful carriages waiting, with their scarlet outriders, and in a quarter of an hour the flag was lowered, and the Court Circular announced, "Her Majesty left the palace at twenty minutes past three;" and I went off in the rain to the Klingemanns, and had the double pleasure of pouring out all my news to them and to Cécile.—It was a happy morning.

I must add that I begged the Queen to allow me to dedicate my A minor symphony to her, as that had really been the inducement of my journey, and because the English name on the Scotch piece would look doubly well. Also, I forgot to tell you how just as she was going to begin to sing she said, "But the parrot must go out first, or he will screech louder than I shall sing;" upon which Prince Albert rang the bell, and the Prince of Gotha said he would carry it out, and I said "Allow me," and carried the great cage out, to the astonishment of the servants. There is plenty more to say when we meet; but if Dirichlet goes and thinks me a little aristocrat because of this long history, I swear I am more radical than ever, and call to witness Grote, Roebuck, and you, my dear little mother, who will be as much amused by all these details as I am myself.

As I am in the midst of descriptions I must speak of one thing more—how after a splendid crossing we heard in the night that we were only half an hour from Ostend, and I went up on deck and found a calm grey sea, morning just breaking, lovely stars, and the steamer making straight for the lighthouse, which gleamed out all white and bright, with a couple of red and yellow lights down below to show where the pier was; and England lay behind us, and the Continent, which is also beautiful, before us.

On the Rhine we unhappily received the terrible news from France. No doubt you also, like all of us, were deeply grieved at the young man's * sad fate.

---

* Louis Philippe's eldest son, the Duke of Orleans, killed at Neuilly by the overturning of his carriage, on the 13th of July, 1842.

With James I did not make acquaintance (and I confess my ignorance unwillingly), and saw his name for the first time in your letter.

Again I say a thousand, thousand thanks for your dear letter, and I beg and pray for more and for many. I am no flatterer when I say what a delight such a letter from you is for all of us, and how earnestly we long for speedy and frequent news from you,—it is the truth. Do give us this pleasure as often as you possibly can, dear mother. Give my best love to all at home (I mean my sisters and brother, and brothers-in-law, and nephews), and tell them to think nicely of me and to write to me sometimes. Hoping for a happy meeting,

I am always, dear Mother, your

FELIX.

(3.) *To* HERR ————.*

(Translation.)

LEIPZIG, *April* 2, 1843.

MY DEAR SIR,

A thousand thanks for your kind letter, and for the fact of your being one of those people who do not look upon the memories of pleasant times and happy days as dead, but rather as a living and active influence, just as I do with my whole heart, and have

* The original has neither name nor address.

insisted on all my life! Every little circumstance which you mention, and a vast number of smaller ones besides, such as the places we sat in at Erard's, and the lights which were burned at the Baillot-Soirée, and the parts on the blue paper, and the tea which we drank before it began—all this came upon me as if it were yesterday, when I got your letter with its greetings from happy past times. It is just because such things remain so unforgotten, so dear and precious to me, and because most people like to forget the past in the present, that I am doubly glad when some one thinks as I do, and takes the past with the present, and rejoices in it—and so I thank you with all my heart for your letter; and especially for the dear kind remembrance which you have kept of me with all these details, and for the assurance that you have not lost the good friendship of those days for me, and will not lose it. That it is the same with me you know very well, and so I join with you most heartily in the wish that we may soon meet one another once again in the world and be happy together. Then we will revel in all the recollections of that Paris life, and see who can outdo the other in them, and above all we will add others to them, new and delightful ones of the time being, and make new experiences which shall also last out their twelve years, fresh and vivid. Only let it be soon, whether in Leipzig, or at Ausbach, or on the way anywhere else about in Germany.—Herr Dürrner, whose talent I value very highly, I have unfortunately seen but once here, and that for a very short time. My winter-months are so completely filled up with work, both public and private, that I do not have the least time for social intercourse. So I shall enjoy it all the more after Easter, when all my public duties cease for six months. I rejoice immensely in that time, and hope that I may then see a great deal of Herr Dürrner, and get to know his compositions thoroughly, and become as intimately acquainted with him and his music as a superficial acquaintance has already made me wish to be. I also hope to hear plenty more details from him about you and your life there, and then he will be able to report to you about me and my life. But the best thing, as I said before, would be that we should do it for ourselves, and so be able to judge at once with our own eyes.

In the hope that this wish may soon be fulfilled, and with many thanks for your kind remembrances and friendly letter, I must close this, and remain, with great respect, always yours faithfully,

FELIX MENDELSSOHN BARTHOLDY.

II.

(4.) To W. Sterndale Bennett, Esq.*

(Original.)

Leipzig, *April* 3, 1839.

.... You are now in the middle of your London season, with concerts, foreigners, businesses &c. of every kind and you will be giddy and occupied enough I dare say; and yet I write these lines in order to increase your occupations if possible, to add a new trouble to those that already surround you, in short to ask a question—perhaps also a favour. You will recollect that I had a mind to publish some of Handel's Scores, viz. in the original shape, and only with a written Organ part of mine, for those that do not know how to accompany that sort of music on the organ.

..... Since your departure Breitkopf and Härtel have readily undertaken to publish three oratorios in Score as a beginning and to go on with it if the Public takes interest in the matter.

Now after I looked over my Arnold's Edition I find it so full of mistakes so far from accurate in the details that it is impossible to give a new edition without comparing the manuscripts which are in your King's

---

* From the original in the possession of Sir W. Sterndale Bennett.

(or Queen's) library and the other editions of Handel which may exist. My Question then is: will you do me the favor to assist me in that undertaking, by looking over the M.S. in those parts which appear doubtful in Arnold's Edition, by comparing the other editions when the M.S. does not explain the questioned passages, or by asking advice of those English musicians whom you think best acquainted with Handelian music and spirit, if the matter still remains undecided. I know your kindness and that if you are not too occupied and your time not too much taken up by the season you will answer in the affirmative. Allow me then to add a few questions which the perusal of Arnold's score of Samson (which is to be amongst the three) suggested to my mind, and which you would greatly oblige me in answering. I saw the original of Samson in the King's library in 1829 and Mr. Anderson gave me then the permission to look it over and take memoranda.

I. Are the Cyphers (how do you call it?, Bezifferung, the numbers that indicate the chords in the bass part) Handel's or whose else?

Are there any Cyphers in the manuscript?

II. Do you ever play the organ in England to Handel's overtures, as for instance to that of Samson?

III. In some oratorios I find songs and recitatives

which are evidently not to be sung one after the other, but only composed to give a choice to the singer so that only one out of many must be performed. Several instances occur in Arnold's Edition of the Messiah. But also in Samson there are many songs which seem rather out of keeping, and some repetitions which look as if they were only to give a choice, not to be performed one after the other. Are there any proofs of the truth of this to be found in the manuscript? For instance in the beginning where the three airs are in A, D, and B minor, with the chorus in D are repeated three times, seem rather doubtful? But more so the two dead marches, one after the other, one in C and one in D? Is there no indication which was the original one? Also the repetition of the Chorus of Virgins page 89 of Arnold, after it came in already page 88. Also (but for other reasons) Dalila's songs page 79 and 91; also the Recitative, 6th Bar, page 30; Song page 40; ditto page 61; 62; 69 and 70; and page 97 &c. &c. &c.

IV. Is there no indication of "Presto" in Handel's handwriting in the chorus "O first created beam" when the words "to thy dark servant" begin?

V. Is there another edition of the Score of Samson than Arnold's?

VI. In page 46 of Arn. Ed. there are the 4 beginning bars of the Recit. without Accomp.; it comes afterwards in, nobody knows how. Is that also the case in the manuscript?

And if you find other things which strike you when comparing the MS. with the printed Copy pray let me know them.

Now excuse all that trouble and let me have an answer as soon as possible. Tell me how you are, now you find yourself in England again. . . . .

I shall stay here till the 23rd of this month; from then till the end of May direct any communications to Düsseldorf, poste restante; from the beginning of June to Frankfort, poste restante. . . . . Farewell.

F. M. B.

(5.) *To* G. A. MACFARREN, ESQ., *London.*

(Original.)

LEIPZIG, 2nd April, 1843.

MY DEAR SIR,

You have expected a letter from me, and I one from you; for at the conclusion of your last you said you would look out once more for your Overture and send me word, as soon as you had found it. I thought it impossible that such a work should have been lost entirely, and waited every day for the score or some news from you—and now it seems you did the same. When I did not hear from you, I tried to bring out the Symphony in one of our last Concerts, but as I suspected, when I first wrote to you, there was some opposition from the Directors, merely because there had been four new Symphonies in the course of the last two months, and they did so much that I was obliged to postpone it until the beginning of the next season, although it was half copied already. I am sorry you feel disappointed by the delay, but it was not in my power to help it. Meanwhile I must repeat what I said in my first letter—if you *had* an Overture I am sure it would be a better beginning for this public and these Concerts, than a Symphony. Ask Bennett, who knows the place, and who will certainly concur in this opinion. And if you could accordingly let us have an Overture *before* the Symphony, I am sure the last would be much better understood and received by the public, even if there had not been such a quantity of new native Symphonies beforehand, as there has been this year. You tell me, you never wrote an Overture to Rob Roy. But did I dream of it, or what else can it be? for I recollect the key, D major, the time 6-8, recollect that I saw it published, arranged as a duet, that it began with this rhythm: &c., that on the first page of music was printed once more the title—Overture to &c. by A. Macfarren—now can I have invented, or dreamt all this? I wish I was right and you would send it or anything else like it,—for I liked it very much, and so would the people here.*

And as for my not writing, you must never be angry with me for that, or I should be afraid of losing your good opinion very soon. I often live many months without being able to write a letter, sometimes also without an hour of leisure for doing so, and all my friends know it and must bear with it, for it is stronger than I am. Ask Bennett also in this respect.

And as for those good friends of yours who think, as you say, that English music is a thing which cannot be endured in Germany, and that a work of yours would be here like an apparition of two moons,—pray ask them to wait a few months, before they repeat an opinion equally creditable to us and to you, or pray tell them in my name that they are sadly mistaken, and that the event will soon prove them to be so.

I wish I could write much longer, but again I cannot, and can only assure you that I shall always remain

Yours very truly,
FELIX MENDELSSOHN BARTHOLDY.

* Mendelssohn here refers to the Overture to Chevy Chase, which was performed on the 1st November following. See the next letter.

(6.) *To the Same.*

(Original.)

LEIPZIG, 20*th Nov.*, 1843.

MY DEAR SIR,

I am going to leave Leipzig in a few days with wife and children, and chairs and tables and Piano and everything. And while I think of the duties I have still to fulfil as part of the direction of the Abonnement-Concerts, I feel that I must write a few words to you, although I charged Mr. Wessel some time ago to do so in my name. I must tell you that your Overture went very well and was most cordially and unanimously received by the public; that the amateurs hailed it as a work which promised them a great many treats to come, and which gave them such a treat already in itself; that the orchestra played it with true delight and enthusiasm; in short that it is sure to be a favourite with all of them. I rehearsed and conducted it with the utmost care; but now I am going to Berlin and shall not have the pleasure of introducing some of your other Pieces to the Public this winter. But I left the whole of your music with the Concert-Directors (in the hands of Mr. H. C. Schleinitz) who will forward it back to you after the end of the season, and they promised me that they will bring out at least one of your other works, if not several in the course of this winter. Most probably it will be the Symphony, of which the parts are half copied already.

God bless you, my dear Sir; excuse these hasty lines; they pack up all my things and I am in a black, or at least greyish mood. Yes, God bless you from all my heart, and be as happy in your life and in your art as I shall always wish you to be! Very truly yours,

FELIX MENDELSSOHN BARTHOLDY.

(7.) *To the Same.*
(Original.)

4, HOBART PLACE, EATON SQUARE,
June 6th, 1844.

MY DEAR SIR,

I need not tell you with how great a pleasure I would have played your Sonata* to-morrow, if I possibly could—for I hope you know this. And you also know that it is with true and sincere regret that I must say I am not able to undertake the task which you propose me. During the bustle of the last weeks I have not yet been able to become acquainted with your Sonata; the whole of this day and of to-morrow morning is taken up with different musical and un-

* "Ma cousine;" second Sonata (for Pianoforte solo in A); dedicated to Miss Emma Bendixen, by G. Alexander MacFarren.

musical engagements and accordingly I would hardly have an hour till to-morrow night to play your Sonata over. This I cannot think sufficient, and I would not be able to do it justice *in my own eyes*. Do not misunderstand me and take this for false modesty; I know very well that I should be able to-morrow to play it through without stopping and perhaps without wrong notes; but I attach too much importance to any public performance to believe that sufficient, and unless I am myself thoroughly acquainted with a Composition of such importance and compass I would never venture to play it in public. Once more I need not tell you how much I regret it, for you must know it very well.

Mr. Davison told me the Concert was now to begin with my Trio:* I shall therefore be punctually with you to-morrow evening at ½ past 8. I beg you will arrange about having a *good* Piano of Erard's at the room; they know there already which I like best.

Always very sincerely yours,
FELIX MENDELSSOHN BARTHOLDY.

The performance of Mendelssohn's Antigone which formed the occasion of the following letter

* In D minor: Op. 49.

took place early in 1845 at Covent Garden Theatre, where that work was produced for the first time in this country, under the musical direction of Mr. G. A. Macfarren. The enterprise was perfectly successful, and the piece ran thirty nights, only stopping with the termination of the season.

(8.) To the Same.
(Original.)

My dear Sir,   Frankfurt, <i>8th December</i>, 1844.

Your letter came two days before my departure from Berlin, and immediately after it I received the news of the very very sore illness of my youngest child, which called me in great haste back to this place, where I had left my family. The child continues very ill, and the physicians give us but a very faint hope; they say that if it recovers it can only be very slowly, and may last many months, so I need not beg your pardon for not having answered punctually, although the object of your letter was of great musical importance to me. But I say the same words as you do at the end of your letter; and although I love my art, more from my heart indeed than words can say, there are other things before which even that love must vanish and be silent. Do not let me add another word. . . . .

Have many thanks for the interest you take in bringing out my music to the Antigone-Choruses; I am very glad it is in your hands, because it wants a musician like you to make it go as intended—quite as a subordinate part of the whole, as a mere link in the chain of the poem, and yet perfectly clear and independent in itself. I am glad you have so many Chorus-singers; I think they will be necessary in your large Theatre. I hope you will also have them placed not on the stage but in the place where usually the Orchestra is, viz. before the stage, so as it was in Berlin, Dresden, &c., and I believe also at Paris. It enhances the effects of the voices, the distinctness of the words, and the beauty of the scenery most wonderfully. Pray let them pronounce the words as distinctly as possible, so as to make the notes *less* prominent and the words *more* so, than they usually are in Opera-Choruses. Then let the succession of Dialogue and Music be as rapid as possible, indeed quite without the least interruption or pause; for instance when the curtain rises and Antigone has appeared, has called her sister and brought her forward from the background, it must be the last bar but one of the Overture, so that imme-

diately after the last chord of the wind instruments
(G ♮) Antigone begins to speak *while* the chord is still
kept. Again the first Chorus must begin as soon as
Antigone has gone down the steps (not immediately
after Ismene's last words of course), and Kreon must
be seen immediately when the C major chord, *fortissimo*, comes down before the Recitative of the Choruses,
and Kreon must again begin to speak while the chord
E flat is hardly given, and it must be kept during
the first words—and so on throughout the whole. I
wish the effect of the whole music to be very lively
and yet not too fast, and very majestic and yet not
slow. This applies also particularly to the Chorus-
Recitatives, which if sung by a whole mass of voices
are of a good effect, but they must not drag them,
they must not sing them in time, nor waver in
their way of delivering them; it must be as if they
all did speak the words and understand the meaning now faster now slower as the meaning requires
it and never in a dragging and tiresome way; for
instance the Recitative at the end of the 2nd Chorus
it must be delivered with great energy, and as fast
as a single singer would sing the same words—and
so all of them. If you have but one of your Solo
singers who sings Recitatives well and in a *truly
dramatic* way, you will easily make the whole Chorus

INSTRUCTIONS FOR PERFORMANCE.

follow him, and after few Rehearsals they will do it altogether and by themselves. In the Melodramas, where the words must go together with the notes (with Flutes and Clarinets, &c.), do not let the actress take the tempo of your music (as I heard them do lately at Dresden), but let the flutes accompany *her* tempo of speaking, which is also not difficult if the flutes will follow *you* and *her*. When the Chorus answers the speaker in the Melodramas again there must not be the least interruption or pause, and their singing must come in immediately after the last word spoken, while the preceding chord of the Orchestra must already have been heard during the last phrase. Then there is the *acting* of the choruses, which is still important. They must but very seldom (as for instance during the Solo in Quartet in G) be *quite* without motion, and then also they must stand in *groups, not* in the usual theatrical *rows;* but this I hope will have been well managed in France, from where you have the direction I believe. For example, at the beginning of Chorus 1, the singers must not be seen before the 1st chord, then they must come two by two, while they sing the beginning and must wander quickly round the altar during the whole of the 4-4, but when the 2-4 begins they must be in their places; and the singers of the 2d chorus must also not be seen, but after the end of this 2-4, when they come in quite in the same way and do the same as the others &c. &c. The acting of the Chorus to Bacchus in D must be very lively towards the end, when those who sing "Hear us, Bacchus" must always wave their sticks and even go up the steps of the altar the last time, while the others who continue with the other words may stand in a row in front (in the background) until their turn comes to sing "Hear us, Bacchus," when the order is reversed, until it ends with a very animated group round the Altar, which is disturbed by the messenger &c. &c.

Pray excuse this long analysis; but you would have it! And as for Israel and the other copy of the works, do you not think you could find an opportunity for sending them to me at this place! I intend to stay here till next Autumn, if all goes as I wish it; and there are so many of your countrymen, who visit this part of Germany! I also hope to send you the King of Saxony's name as a Subscriber to the Society very shortly, but I must have a prospectus first, and could not get one at Dresden. Pray send me one, and I hope to arrange the matter directly and easily. Did your negociations with Messrs. Breitkopf and Härtel about the Handel Society lead to no result?

But enough. Believe me always yours,
                    FELIX MENDELSSOHN BARTHOLDY.

III.

The following seven letters refer to the Full Score of Handel's "Israel in Egypt," which Mendelssohn edited, with an Organ part of his own, for the "Handel Society"—instituted in April 1843. Mendelssohn collated an old printed copy of "Israel" with the autograph of the work at Buckingham Palace, wrote the proposed organ part, arranged a pianoforte accompaniment for use in the absence of the orchestra, and submitted the complete copy to the Council of the Society on the 8th of July, 1845. During the correction of the proofs, the Council were very persistent in requiring uniformity as to details with those that had already been issued. One of these points resulted in the following minute, dated June 30, 1864 :—" Letters were produced from Sir H. Bishop, Signor Pistrucci, and Count Pepoli; and several other authorities were adduced as to the gender and the con-

struction of the plural of the word 'Oboe.'"
It was consequently resolved, "That the authorities before the meeting leave no doubt that the word 'Oboe' is masculine, and that the termination of the plural is the same as the singular. The word shall therefore be always thus employed in the future productions of the Society, and the instances where it has been hitherto falsely declined shall be corrected in the plates." In Letter No. 11 Mendelssohn alludes to this important subject, which had been long under discussion.

(9.) *To the* HANDEL SOCIETY.
(Original.)

FRANKFORT, 1*st March*, 1845.

GENTLEMEN,
Yesterday I received the King of Saxony's answer, saying that he will become a subscriber to the Handel Society, and that he has sent an order to his Embassy in London to pay the annual subscription for him. Most probably they will also forward the copies of those works that are already published and of the future publications to the King.

Some months ago when my friend Klingemann passed by this place I had just received a letter from Messrs. Breitkopf & Härtel about the Handel Society, stating the difficulty of getting the copies over without much expence to the subscribers, and that this was the great drawback to the undertaking in Germany. I talked the matter over with my friend, and asked him whether Mr. Bunsen, the Prussian Ambassador, who is himself one of Handel's greatest admirers, and has so often opportunities for sending large packages and parcels to this country, could not find a way for sending copies belonging to German subscribers to *some* place in Germany, either Hamburgh, or Cologne, or any other (for the postage from *there* would be no matter). My friend thought it very probable that Mr. Bunsen might offer his assistance in such a way and I thought it my duty to inform you of this, and leave it to you, whether you will talk over this matter with Mr. Klingemann (4, Hobart Place, Eaton Square) and enquire *through him* at Mr. Bunsen's, which I think better than a direct question. At any rate Mr. Bunsen would forward those copies which belong to the King of Prussia, and the Cathedral Society at Berlin (and also pay the subscription for these two, I dare say). They were ordered by *Count Redern*, to whom I applied for it at Berlin.

Finally let me ask you to send me the proofs of

Israel in Egypt, if you possibly can, in the course of the next 3 months. I remain here till July and have much leisure to correct them accurately just now, besides it is much easier for you to send them over here than to any other place in Germany where I may go to hereafter.

I therefore hope you will comply with my request if you possibly can, and am, Gentlemen,

Your most Obedient Servant,

FELIX MENDELSSOHN BARTHOLDY.

(10.) *To* WILLIAM STERNDALE BENNETT, ESQ.*

(Translation.)

FRANKFURT A.M. 26 *May* 1845.

MY DEAR BENNETT,

Many thanks for your kind letter—ach nein, ich will lieber Deutsch schreiben. [The letter then proceeds in German, of which the following is a translation.]

Now I have a request, dear Bennett, with which I certainly ought not to come in the middle of a London Season, but which I still make because I hope you are not too much worried, and you will do me a great

---

* From the original in the possession of Sir W. Sterndale Bennett.

"ISRAEL IN EGYPT."

kindness thereby. Would you get Mr. Anderson to show you Handel's original MS. of Israel in Egypt,* and look at a few notes in it about which I am doubtful, and write me a line about it? These doubtful notes are as follows:—(1) In the Hailstone Chorus, the first note which the *second trumpet has to play*, is it in Handel A or G? (2) In the third chorus after that, "But as for his people," *the fourth note before the close*, is it in the viola D or E? [♪♪♪]? or [♪♪♪]? (3) In the following chorus, "Egypt was glad," *in the sixth bar before the close*, is the second violin so [♪♪♪]? or [♪♪♪]? (4) In the chorus, "But the waters overwhelmed them," *the second note in the 9th bar before the close*, is it in the second violin D or E flat? [♪♪]?

If it is possible for you, pray answer me these four questions—but don't be angry with me. When I think of your Concert on the 24th of June I declare I would rather withdraw my whole request. ; . . .

Hoping that we may soon meet again,

    Always your

        FELIX MENDELSSOHN BARTHOLDY.

---

* In the Royal Library at Buckingham Palace.

(11.) *To* G. A. MACFARREN, ESQ.

(Original.)

LEIPZIG, 28*th September* 1845.

MY DEAR SIR,

I received the proofs of the 2nd Act of Israel, the day before yesterday (with your letter dated 6th July) and as you referred me in your letter of the 2nd Sept. to these proofs, I was not able to return an answer before I had received them. Now I receive to-day your last letter of the 22nd, and hasten to write, although my leisure time of this summer is now over, and I can only write in great hurry, which I beg you will excuse.

The alterations of which you tell me may be made, as they relate to mere matters of form, and I will alter the Preface accordingly. Therefore the titles of the several pieces may stand as a heading to each in the 1st Act, in the same manner you have marked in the proofs of the 2nd. Then the footnotes page 1, 22 and 192 may be expunged and I shall confine them (and those I may have to make still for the 2nd Act) to the preface. The Hautboys may also be called girls instead of boys, although the Dictionary which I carefully consulted before I made the correction most distinctly said the word Oboe was masculine. Never mind all these things, and you may have the 1st part printed as soon as you like.

But pray *be sure* that no more alterations be introduced, and at any rate *not one* with which I am not *previously acquainted,* (may they relate to matters of form or not, to the text of the music or to the PREFACE).

I am busily correcting the proofs of the 2nd Act every free hour I can find. I hope to have done with it in the course of next week, and shall then immediately send it to Mess. Hüttner at Hamburgh for Mr. Buxton, your Auditor.

I have only time to add my best thanks for the great trouble you have again taken on my account with the 2nd part, but I shall write you at length (particularly an answer to the last part of your letter, which interests me very much and which I shall endeavour to answer at once satisfactorily) and privately when I send back the 2d. part proofs. Excuse these hasty lines;

Always yours very truly,
FELIX MENDELSSOHN BARTHOLDY.

(12.) *To the Same.*

(Original.)

LEIPZIG, *October* 1845.

MY DEAR SIR,

I have finished the corrections of the 2d part of Israel, and send it to you with this letter. There are so many faults in it, that a good and exact edition can only be obtained if you will have the kindness to use the utmost care in examining the places where the corrections are made in the plates. I hope you will do me this favour; for if not I should despair of the edition becoming a good one, and should consider the time which I devoted to it (and now even with much difficulty) as entirely lost, or worse than that. There are many places where the engraver arbitrarily deviated from the copy which I prepared with the greatest care for this edition, and where these deviations become faults. This is the case on the very first page of the second part; as it stands engraved, nobody could guess that the "Organo" is meant to play the first C, and to have the subsequent pauses; besides on the 2nd page the staff for the "Organo" would come in without an inscription, and nobody would know what it means; then the 1st page would look as if the Violoncelli had to play those notes alone, and the Contra-Bassi only the first C—in short the whole thing is one confusion, —is *wrong* by the deviation from the old copy which is quite distinct and right. This will be easily altered, but a more difficult and expensive alteration will be necessary for the Chorus, "And I will exalt him," p. 197-208. I wrote the reasons why I cannot allow this deviation under the beginning of that Chorus; the mistake at the beginning and page 203, 204, &c., are quite ridiculous, and as much as I regret to give the engraver and the Society so much trouble I cannot help it, and he must engrave it with *one line* (for Organo and Bassi) while he must engrave the first page of the second part with *two lines*. Another correction which I had to make through the whole of the Oratorio, and which I cannot allow to stand, although it *seems* most insignificant, is the constant use of slurs which the engraver always placed over two notes (quavers or semi-quavers generally) which are to be sung on one word (for instance page 216, bar 4, 6, 8, page 340, bar 2, &c.). I say it *seems* insignificant, but it IS NOT, as I am sure that slurs are used in such cases (in ancient, particularly in Bach's and Handel's, music) as a characteristic sign for the expression, much as we would use this sign:

If such a pause is *not* meant, they do not place the slur over the notes, because it is *quite unnecessary*, the manner of uniting the quavers and semiquavers (♫ ♫, instead of ♬♬) indicating clearly enough that they are to be sung on the same syllable. Another thing which must be carefully done is to add always "by the Editor," to that part of "Organo" which is *mine;* if this is omitted, the misunderstandings which already exist about Handel's Organ parts will be increased to a most fearful extent, notwithstanding the explanation in the Preface: people will believe he has written two, or he has written mine, or he has written none, or I do not know what. Therefore pray be sure this explanation is *never* omitted in the score (also not in the first part, I hope, where I carefully added it when I corrected it). Many faults have also occurred in the Pianoforte adaptation; although I did not receive the Original of this I believe that the greater part of them are *my* faults not the engraver's, and I beg his and your pardon for it, but hope nevertheless that they will be most carefully corrected. The same with the Organo (by the Editor) of which I did not receive the most important pieces (inlaid leaves) and which I wish to be as correct as possible, because I bear the responsibility of it.

Now, my dear Sir, I come to those places where you indicated to me the suggestions of the Council. I wrote my answers under your remarks to save time, but I beg you *will erase the whole* (remarks and answers) before you give the Copy into the Engraver's hands, because I really should not like anybody but you to become acquainted with these things. Indeed the reasons I give are most especially *for you* and for nobody else, and if *that* had not been the case, I would have plainly said that so and so was my opinion, (because nobody shared the responsibility of an Edition which bears my name). It was painful to me not to be able to agree with the Council in some of their suggestions, you will see in looking over the Preface (as altered now) that I have done whatever I could, in introducing all those alterations which relate to the English language (of which I cannot judge) and others which have, to my opinion, the greater probability. But in those cases in which I am of a different opinion I *could not* adopt the reading of the Council (although the difference may only consist in trifles) and as I have not been able to change my opinion in these cases, after duly considering and sincerely wishing it, I beg the Corrections will stand as marked by me in this Copy.

Indeed I must rely on your complying with this wish of mine, for I cannot give my name to anything (and if it was but a trifling thing) which I do not consider right and true myself at that moment. The same is the case with the Preface. I have altered as much as I could; if other things must still be altered for the sake of a good English style (although nobody expects such a thing from me) tell me so, and we will again correspond on this eternal and not very pleasant and musical subject. But do not introduce in the Preface nor in the Score any alterations with which I did not agree, and which I have not seen first.

I heartily hope you might say "Yes" at once to these my requests, and we might *not* be forced again into this sort of unmusical Correspondence which we both equally dislike, I am sure, and which I should be *most* happy to see at an end.

Very truly yours,
Felix Mendelssohn Bartholdy.

(13.) *To the Same.*
(Original.)

Leipsic, 31 *Dec.* 1845.

My dear Sir,

I received your letter this day week and it is already several days since I sent my answer by way of Hamburgh under your direction to Mess. Ewer & Co. I send this letter now by post, that you may have it still sooner if possible. My answer to your former questions is contained in detail in the Hamburgh letter. To the words about "the narrative which forms the subject" I have no objection and they may be inserted at the head of *the text* of the Oratorio (but not in the Score, or else you must write "Council," or "Ed." or what you like under it). But enough.

Many, many good wishes for your Opera! May it succeed and give you and your friends pleasure and many happy hours in 1846 and 1856 and so on!

Always yours very truly,

FELIX MENDELSSOHN BARTHOLDY.

(14.) *To the Same.*
(Original.)

LEIPSIC, 3rd *April*, 1846.

MY DEAR SIR,

The businesses (musical and others) with which I am surrounded here are so numerous that I am totally unable to write letters. I therefore delivered your enclosures to the Editors here, and in a letter, which I had to write to Mr. Buxton, requested him to answer those points of your letter which you now repeat to me. I do not understand why Mr. Buxton did not communicate to you my answer as I wrote it to him, and I write

now in great haste the same to you. You may send the
money in *any* (safe) way you like—it is not for me to
name any and I leave it to you—if I should propose one
it would be, to pay it to Mr. Buxton who could then
have it paid at Hamburgh to my brother's house, as he
often did—but any other way is equally agreeable to
me. If you have the impression that I wished or
consented to become a Member of the Handel Society,
then of course you may deduct three Guineas for three
years subscription but I beg at the same time you will
send the publications of these 3 years to Mr. Buxton to
keep them for me, as I did not receive one volume till
now. The reasons why you want me to be a subscriber
are very flattering and I thank you for saying so, but
I can only repeat what I wrote already to you on that
subject—that I have already one complete edition and
very many single volumes of Handel's works, and that
I therefore do not intend to have, nor indeed can I find
room for a third Edition in my library. It would therefore not be consistent with truth if my name was kept
in future on the subscribers' lists, without my having
subscribed in reality, which, (I must repeat it) I am
not able to do. . . . . . I am my dear Sir, very
truly yours,

     FELIX MENDELSSOHN BARTHOLDY.

(15.) *To the Same.*

(Original.)

LEIPZIG, 28 *December* 1845.

MY DEAR SIR,

I hasten to reply to your letter (which you wrote to me as Secretary of the Handel Society) and which I received yesterday. Have many, many thanks for the trouble you take in correcting and recorrecting the proofs of Israel in Egypt as you have done; but this obligation I have, (if I am not mistaken) to Mr. Macfarren, and not to the Secretary, and my thanks to you I hope to express better in another and more pleasant letter than this can be.

As I told you in my last letter I wish to end the communications I have had with "the Council" on this subject, and am therefore very glad you tell me that the 6 points about which you question me are to be settled *among us two*, and not to be brought again before any Council. *I rely on your word* in this assurance, for if this was not the case I would only say that I expressed my opinion in my last letter (viz. to give way to everything which regards the English language or my personal authority, and in *none* which regards Handel's authority.) But as *we* have to settle it, I go most willingly through the six points. Pray let it be the last time that I must correspond on this subject.

1. Instead of 'pauses in the Contrabassi' say 'rests' and instead of 'lay before the public' say 'the members' or 'the Society' as you think best.

2. The double bar after the Chorus 'He is my God' must *stand* if it is in Handel's manuscript, and *fall* if it is not in it (for I will neither add nor take out anything for 'uniformity's sake'); I corrected the first (Arnold's) Copy, after which this new Copy was engraved note by note, after Handel's manuscript. If then the double bar is in this (Arnold's) Copy, I think it probable that the same is the case in Handel's. But if you will compare this last, which you can easily I fancy, you will greatly oblige me, and the matter will be settled at once.

3. I am sorry to have given you the trouble of copying out the bass parts of the Chorus "I will exalt him." But I must repeat what I said in my last letter, and none of the reasons you can tell me can satisfy me to go against Handel's manuscript in this case. The rests at the beginning (in the *Bass* part) could be placed there without any doubt, as Handel writes at the beginning 'senza Violins and Bassoons' (although he does *not* mention the *Violoncelli*)—but in the middle of the Chorus, the Violoncelli and Bassoons (Fagotti) might most probably be meant to play the same (Tenore &c.)

notes as the Organ (at least I, for one, would make them play them)—and therefore the rests are *not* justified those. Pray then let the plates be re-engraved.

4. The same with regard to the Contra-bassi at the end of "Thou didst blow," viz. let it be engraved as in Handel's manuscript (in the corrected (Arnold) copy) *without* these Contrabassi. *I know* that the custom is in England to let them play the last Symphony,—but in Germany it is customary to let them play the same thing *throughout the whole Song*, wherever the subject is repeated, (almost continually then) and I like the "effect" of it very much. Who is right? Why not adopt the German reading as well as the English? *I* cannot decide it. Handel is right most probably.

5. I will not write Trombone parts. I wish not to prolong the Correspondence, as I told you, or else I should be tempted to tell you my candid opinion of this "Trombone"-decision of the Council, which you now communicated to me. Perhaps I shall do so in a letter which I shall soon write to you, (not to the Secretary, but the musician).

6. Announce my name without any titles at all.

And now let me not add another word but merely say that I am and remain very truly yours,

FELIX MENDELSSOHN BARTHOLDY.

III.

(16.) *To the* HOFRATH FRIEDRICH ROCHLITZ, *Leipsic.**

(Translation.)

DÜSSELDORF, *February* 25, 1835.

HOCHGEEHRTER HERR HOFRATH,

I am very much obliged to you for your last kind letter, and for the announcement it brings me of the fulfilment of what was formerly but an uncertain hope, as well as for the distinction you have awarded me above other composers,—which is for me the greatest pleasure and honour. You must be aware what a gift you bestow on a musician in such a work, and can therefore imagine how very grateful I am to you for it. The Oratorio on which I am now occupied, will, please God, be finished in about three months; and as soon as I have taken breath again for so important a task, and have finished some things which I must undertake directly afterwards, I shall be delighted to begin another work of the kind. It is true this may not be before next winter, but you say yourself that it need not be written immediately, so I accept your kindness with the utmost gratitude, and am now all eagerness to get your

---

* Autograph in the possession of Madame Preusser, daughter of Rochlitz, and an old and valued friend of Mendelssohn.

next letter, and hear what your subject is. Pray do not leave me long in uncertainty, for what you say about it only makes my impatience the greater; and if the subject be in itself attractive to me, there is hardly any doubt but that your treatment of it must make it still more so.

The subject of my present Oratorio is "St. Paul." It begins with his presence at Stephen's trial; and this, with his persecution of the Church and his conversion as far as the conversation with Ananias, forms the first part; the chief points in his after life—the conversion of the heathen, the worship offered him at Lystra, his imprisonment with Silas, the parting with the elders at Ephesus—constitute the second and last part. It is compiled throughout entirely from the Bible words, and whilst writing it I have felt with renewed pleasure how forcible, how exhaustive, and how harmonious the Scripture language is for music. There is an inimitable force in it, and a rhythm which has often seemed of itself to suggest the music to me. I hope to hear my music for the first time this autumn in Frankfort, performed by the "*Cäcilien-Verein;*" and even though I may find plenty of things in it which I should have to avoid in yours, and many errors and faults, I look forward to it with all my heart. But enough of this, and now I will only add a request for an early answer, which I await with the greatest impatience. Pray receive again my best thanks for your kindness, and accept the esteem and respect of yours faithfully,

FELIX MENDELSSOHN BARTHOLDY.

(17.) *To* MR. J. ALFRED NOVELLO, *London.**
(Original.)

LEIPZIG, *7th April,* 1838.

MY DEAR SIR,

I gave Colonel Chatterton's bandmaster the money, according to your wishes, and hope he arrived in your country, and found his way through the difficulties he must have met with by sea and by land, to Manchester.

I wish I could send you the wished-for composition of the set of words you sent me; but it is altogether impossible for me to do anything in the way of prize composition; I cannot do it, if I would force myself to it; and when I was compelled to do so, when a boy, in competition with my sister and fellow-scholars, my works were always wonders of stupidity—not the tenth part of what I could do otherwise. I think that is the

* From the original in possession of Mr. Novello. Some words in the letter are now illegible.

reason why I felt afterwards such an antipathy to prize-fighting in music, that I made a rule never to participate in it. Excuse me therefore, I should like to do as you wish me if I possibly could.

Breitkopf and Härtel will send you the Pianoforte arrangement of my Psalm* in very short time, and write you about it. They wish to print the full score with the English words, as I think you will publish it in England. Send them the English translation as soon as you have it. I looked at the English Bible and found the words would do with some alteration. These of course must be cleverly made, and at all events I wish you will stick to the words of the Bible as much as you can. Show Mr. Klingemann the translation before you adopt it. I think you will like this Psalm.

As for my old Service which you will publish at present . . . I beg you will write once more about it if you want it, as I must copy it out afresh and could bring it with me and hand it over to you at Cologne. Now you really must come to Cologne,† and your plan of bringing . . . with you and of accepting the prospect of music and . . . is most excellent. Pray do come ; I am so sure you will care for the music. I do not know yet how the performance will go off; we have the

---

* The 42nd Psalm—" As the hart pants." (Op. 42.)
† For the Lower-Rhine music-festival of 1838.

whole festival made up of seldom-performed music;
but there is a glorious Cantata of [Sebastian Bach's]
amongst the number, with a double chorus in it, which
would repay for the journey by itself. And the Rhein-
wein, and [besides] that the whole Oratorio of Joshua.
[Bach's] new Cantata and Cologne's old Cathedral and
the gay green Rhein, I hope you will not resist all these
attractions and be sure to come over; and a most hearty
welcome you shall have. My wife's best compliments;
my boy is a wonderful creature for eating and sleeping,
crying into the bargain; but in excellent health which
is the best of all.

>I am always very truly yours,
> FELIX MENDELSSOHN BARTHOLDY.

(18.) *To* HERR ANTON ZUCCALMAGLIO.
(Translation.)

LEIPZIG, *December* 4, 1839.

HOCHGEEHRTER HERR,

I have long wanted to write and thank you for
your kind letter, and for the beautiful poem, which has
been in my hands since the end of September. Pray
forgive this long delay; in intention I have written
to you many a time, long since, but my days here have

been far too full of interruptions of all sorts, both private and public, pleasant and unpleasant, to allow of my doing it actually.

Now that things are a little quieter my first object is to thank you heartily for all your kindness, especially for this new proof of it, which has given me much pleasure. Your subject is very poetic and beautiful, and your idea of the opposing voices, of the warriors and the maidens, and the disappearance of the latter and their concealment in the rock, is capitally worked out. But I have one objection; it seems to me that in the poem the moment of the actual transformation does not stand out clearly enough, at least one does not clearly understand what becomes of the church and her protégés; and I confess that I cannot quite make out your meaning as to the end of the maidens (in the poem, I mean) whether they are enclosed in the rock, or whether through the transformation they are lifted up "to the gates of Heaven." Or perhaps my objection springs from the whole form of the poem, and could only be removed by a visible transformation? Anyhow I believe even one verse might help to make it clearer; but what do you think?

I would gladly have sent you some music instead of this tiresome letter, but I have so little time to myself in the winter. The Concerts and the whole way of life take up more time and leisure than I expected, and I am glad enough if in my spare time I can but manage to clear up my unfinished work, leaving the beginning of new things for the summer months, which thus become doubly delightful. Is there any chance of your coming to see us again soon? and for longer than last time? Please write me a few lines, and tell me how you are and what you are doing. I should also be so glad to hear something about H. Ernemann, in whose fate I felt much concerned this autumn when he was laid up at Frankfort, and of whom I have since heard nothing. Perhaps you could tell me something about him?

With the greatest esteem,
Ever yours most faithfully,
FELIX MENDELSSOHN BARTHOLDY.

(19.) *To* HERR ADOLF BOETTGER, *Leipsic.*
(Translation.)

BERLIN, *December* 10, 1841.

HOCHGEEHRTER HERR,

Thank you sincerely for your kind letter, which I answer with all the frankness that an object of such great and immediate moment so emphatically demands, provided that it leads us to the end in view, and not away from it. I have frequently thought over the subject of the Legend of St. Genoveva, which you propose, but have always been deterred from it by a certain passiveness in the character or at least in the action of the chief personage. By which I mean that our interest in Genoveva arises more from what she suffers and the way in which she suffers it, than from what she does, or from any dramatic business or action on her part. For her rejection of the importunities of her friend really forms only the starting point of the story, and is certainly not its chief motive, which lies in the suffering she undergoes; and therein I find—what shall I say?—something weak and passive, and in my judgment quite unfit for the material for an opera. I believe that this accounts for the non-success of several attempts to treat the subject. An Opera of that name was given here a short time* since, and was not well received; chiefly, as I am informed, on account of the too uniformly elegiac character of the material. But perhaps you would treat the situations so as to give a different cast to all this? In that case I beg you to give me a very general outline of the way in which you would conceive the course of the business. But I can hardly

---

* Schumann's "Genoveva" was completed in August 1848, and produced at the Leipsic theatre on June 25, 1850. The reference in the text is therefore to some other composition.

believe that even under the liveliest treatment any really active dramatic life could be thrown into the principal personage, or a really original and characteristic development given to the subordinate personages in the piece.

Waiting a reply at your convenience, and with great esteem,

I am, yours faithfully,
FELIX MENDELSSOHN BARTHOLDY.

(20.) *To* PROFESSOR WOLFGANG R. GRIEPENKERL, *Brunswick.*[*]

(Translation.)

BERLIN, *November* 18, 1844.

HOCHGEEHRTER HERR,

Many thanks for your kind letter of the 11th, from which, however, I regret to see that there has been some mistake. My brother-in-law told me a few weeks ago that you had written or were proposing to write a book for an Opera, and asked me if I felt inclined to set it to music. Although I cannot at present undertake an Opera on account of many other works in progress, I said to him that in any case it would interest me much

[*] Autograph in the possession of William Mitchell, Esq.

to make acquaintance with your poem, and that it would afford me great satisfaction if you were inclined to send me an Opera book.

To Shakespeare's "Tempest," as an Opera, I have, I confess, little inclination; nor does the destruction of Jerusalem—at least as I have hitherto seen it treated—appear to me fit for the Theatre. But the fact is that the whole matter depends more on the *how* than the *what*, and that no subject can be either accepted or rejected unconditionally. One important thing appears to me to be that the Composer and the Poet should meet, if only for a short time, so as to talk over and understand the thing. Without that I fear that there can be no real co-operation, and on this ground alone I should like very soon to meet you again.

Hoping that my wish may be fulfilled, and with much consideration,

Yours faithfully,

FELIX MENDELSSOHN BARTHOLDY.

THE END.

LONDON:
R. CLAY, SONS, AND TAYLOR, PRINTERS,
BREAD STREET HILL.

BEDFORD STREET, COVENT GARDEN, LONDON,
April, 1872.

MACMILLAN & CO.'S CATALOGUE of Works in the Departments of History, Biography, and Travels; Politics, Political and Social Economy, Law, etc.; and Works connected with Language. With some short Account or Critical Notice concerning each Book.

HISTORY, BIOGRAPHY, and TRAVELS.

Baker (Sir Samuel W.)—Works by Sir SAMUEL BAKER M.A., F.R.G.S.:—

THE ALBERT N'YANZA Great Basin of the Nile, and Exploration of the Nile Sources. New and Cheaper Edition. Maps and Illustrations. Crown 8vo. 6*s*.

"*Bruce won the source of the Blue Nile; Speke and Grant won the Victoria source of the great White Nile; and I have been permitted to succeed in completing the Nile Sources by the discovery of the great reservoir of the equatorial waters, the Albert N'yanza, from which the river issues as the entire White Nile.*"—PREFACE. "*As a Macaulay arose among the historians,*" *says the* READER, "*so a Baker has arisen among the explorers.*" "*Charmingly written;*" *says the* SPECTATOR, "*full, as might be expected, of incident, and free from that wearisome reiteration of useless facts which is the drawback to almost all books of African travel.*"

THE NILE TRIBUTARIES OF ABYSSINIA, and the Sword Hunters of the Hamran Arabs. With Maps and Illustrations. Fourth and Cheaper Edition. Crown 8vo. 6*s*.

Sir Samuel Baker here describes twelve months' exploration, during which he examined the rivers that are tributary to the Nile from Abyssinia, including the Atbara, Settite, Royan, Salaam, Angrab, Rahad, Dinder, and the Blue Nile. The interest attached to these portions of Africa differs entirely from that of the White Nile regions, as the whole of Upper Egypt and Abyssinia is capable of development, and is inhabited by races having some degree of civilization; while Central Africa is peopled by a race of savages, whose future is more problematical. The TIMES says: "It solves finally a geographical riddle which hitherto had been extremely perplexing, and it adds much to our information respecting Egyptian Abyssinia and the different races that spread over it. It contains, moreover, some notable instances of English daring and enterprising skill; it abounds in animated tales of exploits dear to the heart of the British sportsman; and it will attract even the least studious reader, as the author tells a story well, and can describe nature with uncommon power."

Barante (M. De).—*See* GUIZOT.

Baring-Gould (Rev. S., M.A.)—LEGENDS OF OLD TESTAMENT CHARACTERS, from the Talmud and other sources. By the Rev. S. BARING-GOULD, M.A. Author of "Curious Myths of the Middle Ages," "The Origin and Development of Religious Belief," "In Exitu Israel," &c. In Two Vols. Crown 8vo. 16s. Vol. I. Adam to Abraham. Vol. II. Melchizedek to Zechariah.

Mr. Baring-Gould's previous contributions to the History of Mythology and the formation of a science of comparative religion are admitted to be of high importance; the present work, it is believed, will be found to be of equal value. He has collected from the Talmud and other sources, Jewish and Mohammedan, a large number of curious and interesting legends concerning the principal characters of the Old Testament, comparing these frequently with similar legends current among many of the peoples, savage and civilized, all over the world. "These volumes contain much that is very strange, and, to the ordinary English reader, very novel."—DAILY NEWS.

Barker (Lady).—*See also* BELLES LETTRES CATALOGUE.

STATION LIFE IN NEW ZEALAND. By LADY BARKER Second and Cheaper Edition. Globe 8vo. 3s. 6d.

These letters are the exact account of a lady's experience of the brighter and less practical side of colonization. They record the expeditions, adventures, and emergencies diversifying the daily life of the wife of a New Zealand sheep-farmer; and, as each was written while the novelty and excitement of the scenes it describes were fresh upon her, they may succeed in giving here in England an adequate impression of the delight and freedom of an existence so far removed from our own highly-wrought civilization. "We have never read a more truthful or a pleasanter little book."— ATHENÆUM.

Bernard, St.—*See* MORISON.

Blanford (W. T.)—GEOLOGY AND ZOOLOGY OF ABYSSINIA. By W. T. BLANFORD. 8vo. 21*s*.

This work contains an account of the Geological and Zoological Observations made by the author in Abyssinia, when accompanying the British Army on its march to Magdala and back in 1868, *and during a short journey in Northern Abyssinia, after the departure of the troops. Part I. Personal Narrative; Part II. Geology; Part III. Zoology. With Coloured Illustrations and Geological Map.* "*The result of his labours,*" *the* ACADEMY *says,* "*is an important contribution to the natural history of the country.*"

Bryce.—THE HOLY ROMAN EMPIRE. By JAMES BRYCE, D.C.L., Regius Professor of Civil Law, Oxford. New and Revised Edition. Crown 8vo. 7*s*. 6*d*.

The object of this treatise is not so much to give a narrative history of the countries included in the Romano-Germanic Empire—Italy during the Middle Ages, Germany from the ninth century to the nineteenth—as to describe the Holy Empire itself as an institution or system, the wonderful offspring of a body of beliefs and traditions which have almost wholly passed away from the world. To make such a description intelligible it has appeared best to give the book the form rather of a narrative than of a dissertation; and to combine with an exposition of what may be called the theory of the Empire an outline of the political history of Germany, as well as some notice of the affairs of mediæval Italy. Nothing else so directly linked the old world to the new as the Roman Empire, which exercised over the minds of men an influence such as its material strength could never have commanded. It is of this influence, and the causes that gave it power, that the present work is designed to treat. "*It exactly supplies a want; it affords a key to much which men read of in their books as isolated facts, but of which they have hitherto had no connected exposition set before them. We know of no writer who has so thoroughly grasped the real nature of the mediæval Empire, and its relations alike to earlier and to later times."*—SATURDAY REVIEW.

Burke (Edmund).—*See* MORLEY (JOHN).

Cameos from English History.—*See* YONGE (MISS).

Chatterton.—*See* WILSON (DANIEL).

Cooper.—ATHENÆ CANTABRIGIENSES. By CHARLES HENRY COOPER, F.S.A., and THOMPSON COOPER, F.S.A. Vol. I. 8vo., 1500—85, 18s.; Vol. II., 1586—1609, 18s.

This elaborate work, which is dedicated by permission to Lord Macaulay, contains lives of the eminent men sent forth by Cambridge, after the fashion of Anthony à Wood, in his famous "Athenæ Oxonienses."

Cox (G. V., M.A.)—RECOLLECTIONS OF OXFORD. By G. V. Cox, M.A., New College, late Esquire Bedel and Coroner in the University of Oxford. *Cheaper Edition.* Crown 8vo. 6s.

"An amusing farrago of anecdote, and will pleasantly recall in many a country parsonage the memory of youthful days."—TIMES. *"Those who wish to make acquaintance with the Oxford of their grandfathers, and to keep up the intercourse with Alma Mater during their father's time, even to the latest novelties in fashion or learning of the present day, will do well to procure this pleasant, unpretending little volume."*—ATLAS.

"Daily News."—THE DAILY NEWS CORRESPONDENCE of the War between Germany and France, 1870—1. Edited with Notes and Comments. New Edition. Complete in One Volume. With Maps and Plans. Crown 8vo. 6s.

This Correspondence has been translated into German. In a Preface the Editor says:—

"Among the various pictures, recitals, and descriptions which have appeared, both of our gloriously ended national war as a whole, and of its several episodes, we think that in laying before the German public, through

a translation, the following *War Letters which appeared first in the* DAILY NEWS, *and were afterwards published collectively, we are offering them a picture of the events of the war of a quite peculiar character. Their communications have the advantage of being at once entertaining and instructive, free from every romantic embellishment, and nevertheless written in a vein intelligible and not fatiguing to the general reader. The writers linger over events, and do not disdain to surround the great and heroic war-pictures with arabesques, gay and grave, taken from camp-life and the life of the inhabitants of the occupied territory. A feature which distinguishes these Letters from all other delineations of the war is that they do not proceed from a single pen, but were written from the camps of both belligerents."* " *These notes and comments," according to the* SATURDAY REVIEW, " *are in reality a very well executed and continuous history."*

Dilke.—GREATER BRITAIN. A Record of Travel in English-speaking Countries during 1866-7. (America, Australia, India.) By Sir CHARLES WENTWORTH DILKE, M.P. Fifth Edition. Crown 8vo. 6s.

" *Mr. Dilke," says the* SATURDAY REVIEW, " *has written a book which is probably as well worth reading as any book of the same aims and character that ever was written. Its merits are that it is written in a lively and agreeable style, that it implies a great deal of physical pluck, that no page of it fails to show an acute and highly intelligent observer, that it stimulates the imagination as well as the judgment of the reader, and that it is on perhaps the most interesting subject that can attract an Englishman who cares about his country."* " *Many of the subjects discussed in these pages," says the* DAILY NEWS, " *are of the widest interest, and such as no man who cares for the future of his race and of the world can afford to treat with indifference."*

Dürer (Albrecht).—*See* HEATON (MRS. C.)

European History, Narrated in a Series of Historical Selections from the best Authorities. Edited and arranged by E. M. SEWELL and C. M. YONGE. First Series, crown 8vo. 6s. ; Second Series, 1088-1228, crown 8vo. 6s.

When young children have acquired the outlines of history from abridgments and catechisms, and it becomes desirable to give a more enlarged view of the subject, in order to render it really useful and interesting, a difficulty often arises as to the choice of books. *Two courses are open, either to take a general and consequently dry history of facts, such as Russell's Modern Europe, or to choose some work treating of a particular period or subject, such as the works of Macaulay and Froude. The former course usually renders history uninteresting; the latter is unsatisfactory, because it is not sufficiently comprehensive. To remedy this difficulty, selections, continuous and chronological, have in the present volume been taken from the larger works of Freeman, Milman, Palgrave, Lingard, Hume, and others, which may serve as distinct landmarks of historical reading. "We know of scarcely anything," says the* GUARDIAN, *of this volume, "which is so likely to raise to a higher level the average standard of English education."*

Fairfax (Lord).—A LIFE OF THE GREAT LORD FAIRFAX, Commander-in-Chief of the Army of the Parliament of England. By CLEMENTS R. MARKHAM, F.S.A. With Portraits, Maps, Plans, and Illustrations. Demy 8vo. 16s.

No full Life of the great Parliamentary Commander has appeared; and it is here sought to produce one—based upon careful research in contemporary records and upon family and other documents. "Highly useful to the careful student of the History of the Civil War. . . . Probably as a military chronicle Mr. Markham's book is one of the most full and accurate that we possess about the Civil War."—FORTNIGHTLY REVIEW.

Field (E. W.)—*See* SADLER.

Freeman.—Works by EDWARD A. FREEMAN, M.A., D.C.L.

"That special power over a subject which conscientious and patient research can only achieve, a strong grasp of facts, a true mastery over detail, with a clear and manly style—all these qualities join to make the Historian of the Conquest conspicuous in the intellectual arena."—ACADEMY.

HISTORY OF FEDERAL GOVERNMENT, from the Foundation of the Achaian League to the Disruption of the United States. Vol. I. General Introduction. History of the Greek Federations. 8vo. 21s.

Mr. Freeman's aim, in this elaborate and valuable work, is not so much to discuss the abstract nature of Federal Government, as to exhibit its actual working in ages and countries widely removed from one another. Four Federal Commonwealths stand out, in four different ages of the world, as commanding above all others the attention of students of political history,

Freeman (E. A.)—*continued.*

viz. the Achaian League, the Swiss Cantons, the United Provinces, the United States. *The first volume, besides containing a General Introduction, treats of the first of these. In writing this volume the author has endeavoured to combine a text which may be instructive and interesting to any thoughtful reader, whether specially learned or not, with notes which may satisfy the requirements of the most exacting scholar.* "*The task Mr. Freeman has undertaken,*" *the* SATURDAY REVIEW *says,* "*is one of great magnitude and importance. It is also a task of an almost entirely novel character. No other work professing to give the history of a political principle occurs to us, except the slight contributions to the history of representative government that is contained in a course of M. Guizot's lectures . . . . The history of the development of a principle is at least as important as the history of a dynasty, or of a race.*";

OLD ENGLISH HISTORY. With *Five Coloured Maps.* Second Edition. Extra fcap. 8vo., half-bound. 6s.

"*Its object,*" *the Preface says,* "*is to show that clear, accurate, and scientific views of history, or indeed of any subject, may be easily given to children from the very first. . . . I have throughout striven to connect the history of England with the general history of civilized Europe, and I have especially tried to make the book serve as an incentive to a more accurate study of historic geography.*" *The rapid sale of the first edition and the universal approval with which the work has been received prove the correctness of the author's notions, and show that for such a book there was ample room. The work is suited not only for children, but will serve as an excellent text-book for older students, a clear and faithful summary of the history of the period for those who wish to revive their historical knowledge, and a book full of charms for the general reader. The work is preceded by a complete chronological Table, and appended is an exhaustive and useful Index. In the present edition the whole has been carefully revised, and such improvements as suggested themselves have been introduced.* "*The book indeed is full of instruction and interest to students of all ages, and he must be a well-informed man indeed who will not rise from its perusal with clearer and more accurate ideas of a too much neglected portion of English history.*"—SPECTATOR.

HISTORY OF THE CATHEDRAL CHURCH OF WELLS, as illustrating the History of the Cathedral Churches of the Old Foundation. Crown 8vo. 3s. 6d.

Freeman (E. A.)—*continued.*

'*I have here,*" *the author says,* "*tried to treat the history of the Church of Wells as a contribution to the general history of the Church and Kingdom of England, and specially to the history of Cathedral Churches of the Old Foundation. . . . I wish to point out the general principles of the original founders as the model to which the Old Foundations should be brought back, and the New Foundations reformed after their pattern.*" "*The history assumes in Mr. Freeman's hands a significance, and, we may add, a practical value as suggestive of what a cathedral ought to be, which make it well worthy of mention.*"—SPECTATOR.

HISTORICAL ESSAYS. Second Edition. 8vo. 10s. 6d.

The principle on which these Essays have been chosen is that of selecting papers which refer to comparatively modern times, or, at least, to the existing states and nations of Europe. By a sort of accident a number of the pieces chosen have thrown themselves into something like a continuous series bearing on the historical causes of the great events of 1870—71. *Notes have been added whenever they seemed to be called for; and whenever he could gain in accuracy of statement or in force or clearness of expression, the author has freely changed, added to, or left out, what he originally wrote. To many of the Essays has been added a short note of the circumstances under which they were written. It is needless to say that any product of Mr. Freeman's pen is worthy of attentive perusal; and it is believed that the contents of this volume will throw light on several subjects of great historical importance and the widest interest. The following is a list of the subjects:*—1. The Mythical and Romantic Elements in Early English History; 2. The Continuity of English History; 3. The Relations between the Crowns of England and Scotland; 4. Saint Thomas of Canterbury and his Biographers; 5. The Reign of Edward the Third; 6. The Holy Roman Empire; 7. The Franks and the Gauls; 8. The Early Sieges of Paris; 9. Frederick the First, King of Italy; 10. The Emperor Frederick the Second; 11. Charles the Bold; 12. Presidential Government. "*He never touches a question without adding to our comprehension of it, without leaving the impression of an ample knowledge, a righteous purpose, a clear and powerful understanding.*"—SATURDAY REVIEW.

THE GROWTH OF THE ENGLISH CONSTITUTION FROM THE EARLIEST TIMES. In the press.

HISTORY, BIOGRAPHY, & TRAVELS.

Galileo.—THE PRIVATE LIFE OF GALILEO. Compiled principally from his Correspondence and that of his eldest daughter, Sister Maria Celeste, Nun in the Franciscan Convent of S. Matthew in Arcetri. With Portrait. Crown 8vo. 7s. 6d.

It has been the endeavour of the compiler to place before the reader a plain, ungarbled statement of facts; and, as a means to this end, to allow Galileo, his friends, and his judges to speak for themselves as far as possible. All the best authorities have been made use of, and all the materials which exist for a biography have been in this volume put into a symmetrical form. The result is a most touching picture skilfully arranged of the great heroic man of science and his devoted daughter, whose letters are full of the deepest reverential love and trust, amply repaid by the noble soul. The SATURDAY REVIEW *says of the book,* "*It is not so much the philosopher as the man who is seen in this simple and life-like sketch, and the hand which portrays the features and actions is mainly that of one who had studied the subject the closest and the most intimately. This little volume has done much within its slender compass to prove the depth and tenderness of Galileo's heart.*"

Gladstone (Right Hon. W. E., M.P.)—JUVENTUS MUNDI. The Gods and Men of the Heroic Age. Crown 8vo. cloth. With Map. 10s. 6d. Second Edition.

This work of Mr. Gladstone deals especially with the historic element in Homer, expounding that element and furnishing by its aid a full account of the Homeric men and the Homeric religion. It starts, after the introductory chapter, with a discussion of the several races then existing in Hellas, including the influence of the Phœnicians and Egyptians. It contains chapters on the Olympian system, with its several deities; on the Ethics and the Polity of the Heroic age; on the Geography of Homer; on the characters of the Poems; presenting, in fine, a view of primitive life and primitive society as found in the poems of Homer. To this New Edition various additions have been made. "*Seldom,*" *says the* ATHENÆUM, "*out of the great poems themselves, have these Divinities looked so majestic and respectable. To read these brilliant details is like standing on the Olympian threshold and gazing at the ineffable brightness within.*" "*There is,*" *according to the* WESTMINSTER REVIEW, "*probably no other writer now living who could have done the work of this book. . . It would be difficult to point out a book that contains so much fulness of knowledge along with so much freshness of perception and clearness of presentation.*"

Guizot.—M. DE BARANTE, a Memoir, Biographical and Autobiographical. By M. GUIZOT. Translated by the Author of "JOHN HALIFAX, GENTLEMAN." Crown 8vo. 6s. 6d.

"*It is scarcely necessary to write a preface to this book. Its lifelike, portrait of a true and great man, painted unconsciously by himself in his letters and autobiography, and retouched and completed by the tender hand of his surviving friend—the friend of a lifetime—is sure, I think, to be appreciated in England as it was in France, where it appeared in the Revue de Deux Mondes. Also, I believe every thoughtful mind will enjoy its clear reflections of French and European politics and history for the last seventy years, and the curious light thus thrown upon many present events and combinations of circumstances.*"—PREFACE. "*The highest purposes of both history and biography are answered by a memoir so lifelike, so faithful, and so philosophical.*"—BRITISH QUARTERLY REVIEW. "*This eloquent memoir, which for tenderness, gracefulness, and vigour, might be placed on the same shelf with Tacitus' Life of Agricola. . . . Mrs. Craik has rendered the language of Guizot in her own sweet translucent English.*"—DAILY NEWS.

Heaton (Mrs. C.)—HISTORY OF THE LIFE OF ALBRECHT DÜRER, of Nürnberg. With a Translation of his Letters and Journal, and some account of his Works. By Mrs. CHARLES HEATON. Royal 8vo. bevelled boards, extra gilt. 31s. 6d.

This work contains about Thirty Illustrations, ten of which are productions by the Autotype (carbon) process, and are printed in permanent tints by Messrs. Cundall and Fleming, under licence from the Autotype Company, Limited; the rest are Photographs and Woodcuts.

Hole.—A GENEALOGICAL STEMMA OF THE KINGS OF ENGLAND AND FRANCE. By the Rev. C. HOLE, M.A., Trinity College, Cambridge. On Sheet, 1s.

The different families are printed in distinguishing colours, thus facilitating reference.

Hozier (H. M.)—Works by CAPTAIN HENRY M. HOZIER, late Assistant Military Secretary to Lord Napier of Magdala.

THE SEVEN WEEKS' WAR; Its Antecedents and Incidents. *New and Cheaper Edition.* With New Preface, Maps, and Plans. Crown 8vo. 6s.

Hosier (H. M.)—*continued.*

This account of the brief but momentous Austro-Prussian War of 1866 claims consideration as being the product of an eye-witness of some of its most interesting incidents. The author has attempted to ascertain and to advance facts. Two maps are given, one illustrating the operations of the Army of the Maine, and the other the operations from Königgrätz. In the Prefatory Chapter to this edition, events resulting from the war of 1866 are set forth, and the current of European history traced down to the recent Franco-Prussian war, a natural consequence of the war whose history is narrated in this volume. "*Mr. Hozier added to the knowledge of military operations and of languages, which he had proved himself to possess, a ready and skilful pen, and excellent faculties of observation and description. . . . All that Mr. Hozier saw of the great events of the war—and he saw a large share of them—he describes in clear and vivid language.*"—SATURDAY REVIEW. "*Mr. Hozier's volumes deserve to take a permanent place in the literature of the Seven Weeks' War.*"—PALL MALL GAZETTE.

THE BRITISH EXPEDITION TO ABYSSINIA. Compiled from Authentic Documents. 8vo. 9s.

Several accounts of the British Expedition have been published. They have, however, been written by those who have not had access to those authentic documents, which cannot be collected directly after the termination of a campaign. The endeavour of the author of this sketch has been to present to readers a succinct and impartial account of an enterprise which has rarely been equalled in the annals of war. "*This,*" *says the* SPECTATOR, "*will be the account of the Abyssinian Expedition for professional reference, if not for professional reading. Its literary merits are really very great.*"

THE INVASIONS OF ENGLAND. A History of the Past, with Lessons for the Future. In the press.

Huyshe (Captain G. L.)—THE RED RIVER EXPEDITION. By Captain G. L. HUYSHE, Rifle Brigade, late on the Staff of Colonel Sir GARNET WOLSELEY. With Maps. 8vo. 10s. 6d.

This account has been written in the hope of directing attention to the successful accomplishment of an expedition which was attended with more than ordinary difficulties. The author has had access to the official documents of the Expedition, and has also availed himself of the reports on the line of route published by Mr. Dawson, C.E., and by the Typographical Department of the War Office. The statements made may therefore be relied on as accurate and impartial. The endeavour has been made to avoid tiring the general reader with dry details of military movements, and yet not to sacrifice the character of the work as an account of a military expedition. The volume contains a portrait of President Louis Riel, and Maps of the route. The ATHENÆUM calls it "an enduring authentic record of one of the most creditable achievements ever accomplished by the British Army."

Irving.—THE ANNALS OF OUR TIME. A Diurnal of Events, Social and Political, Home and Foreign, from the Accession of Queen Victoria to the Peace of Versailles. By JOSEPH IRVING. Second Edition. 8vo. half-bound. 16s.

Every occurrence, metropolitan or provincial, home or foreign, which gave rise to public excitement or discussion, or became the starting point for new trains of thought affecting our social life, has been judged proper matter for this volume. In the proceedings of Parliament, an endeavour has been made to notice all those Debates which were either remarkable as affecting the fate of parties, or led to important changes in our relations with Foreign Powers. Brief notices have been given of the death of all noteworthy persons. Though the events are set down day by day in their order of occurrence, the book is, in its way, the history of an important and well-defined historic cycle. In these 'Annals,' the ordinary reader may make himself acquainted with the history of his own time in a way that has at least the merit of simplicity and readiness; the more cultivated student will doubtless be thankful for the opportunity given him of passing down the historic stream undisturbed by any other theoretical or party feeling than what he himself has at hand to explain the philosophy of our national story. A complete and useful Index is appended. The Table of Administrations is designed to assist the reader in following the various political changes noticed in their chronological order in the 'Annals.'— In the new edition all errors and omissions have been rectified, 300 pages been added, and as many as 46 occupied by an impartial exhibition of the wonderful series of events marking the latter half of 1870. "We have before us a trusty and ready guide to the events of the past thirty years, available equally for the statesman, the politician, the public writer, and the general reader. If Mr. Irving's object has been to bring before the reader all the most noteworthy occurrences which have happened

since the beginning of her Majesty's reign, he may justly claim the credit of having done so most briefly, succinctly, and simply, and in such a manner, too, as to furnish him with the details necessary in each case to comprehend the event of which he is in search in an intelligent manner."
—TIMES.

Kingsley (Canon).—Works by the Rev. CHARLES KINGSLEY, M.A., Rector of Eversley and Canon of Chester. (For other Works by the same Author, *see* THEOLOGICAL and BELLES LETTRES Catalogues.)

ON THE ANCIEN RÉGIME as it existed on the Continent before the FRENCH REVOLUTION. Three Lectures delivered at the Royal Institution. Crown 8vo. 6s.

These three lectures discuss severally (1) *Caste,* (2) *Centralization,* (3) *The Explosive Forces by which the Revolution was superinduced. The Preface deals at some length with certain political questions of the present day.*

AT LAST: A CHRISTMAS in the WEST INDIES. With nearly Fifty Illustrations. New and Cheaper Edition. Crown 8vo. 10s. 6d.

Mr. Kingsley's dream of forty years was at last fulfilled, when he started on a Christmas expedition to the West Indies, for the purpose of becoming personally acquainted with the scenes which he has so vividly described in "Westward Ho!" These two volumes are the journal of his voyage. Records of natural history, sketches of tropical landscape, chapters on education, views of society, all find their place in a work written, so to say, under the inspiration of Sir Walter Raleigh and the other adventurous men who three hundred years ago disputed against Philip II. the possession of the Spanish Main. "We can only say that Mr. Kingsley's account of a 'Christmas in the West Indies' is in every way worthy to be classed among his happiest productions."—STANDARD.

THE ROMAN AND THE TEUTON. A Series of Lectures delivered before the University of Cambridge. 8vo. 12s.

CONTENTS:—*Inaugural Lecture; The Forest Children; The Dying Empire; The Human Deluge; The Gothic Civilizer; Dietrich's End; The Nemesis of the Goths; Paulus Diaconus; The Clergy and the Heathen; The Monk a Civilizer; The Lombard Laws; The Popes and the Lombards;*

The Strategy of Providence. "He has rendered," says the NONCON-FORMIST, "*good service and shed a new lustre on the chair of Modern History at Cambridge* . . . . *He has thrown a charm around the work by the marvellous fascinations of his own genius, brought out in strong relief those great principles of which all history is a revelation, lighted up many dark and almost unknown spots, and stimulated the desire to understand more thoroughly one of the greatest movements in the story of humanity.*"

Kingsley (Henry, F.R.G.S.)—For other Works by same Author, *see* BELLES LETTRES CATALOGUE.

TALES OF OLD TRAVEL. Re-narrated by HENRY KINGSLEY, F.R.G.S. With *Eight Illustrations* by HUARD. Third Edition. Crown 8vo. 6s.

In this volume Mr. Henry Kingsley re-narrates, at the same time preserving much of the quaintness of the original, some of the most fascinating tales of travel contained in the collections of Hakluyt and others. The CONTENTS *are*—*Marco Polo; The Shipwreck of Pelsart; The Wonderful Adventures of Andrew Battel; The Wanderings of a Capuchin; Peter Carder; The Preservation of the "Terra Nova;" Spitzbergen; D'Erme-nonville's Acclimatization Adventure; The Old Slave Trade; Miles Philips; The Sufferings of Robert Everard; John Fox; Alvaro Nunez; The Foundation of an Empire.* "*We know no better book for those who want knowledge or seek to refresh it. As for the 'sensational,' most novels are tame compared with these narratives.*"—ATHENÆUM. "*Exactly the book to interest and to do good to intelligent and high-spirited boys.*"— LITERARY CHURCHMAN.

Macmillan (Rev. Hugh).—For other Works by same Author, *see* THEOLOGICAL and SCIENTIFIC CATALOGUES.

HOLIDAYS ON HIGH LANDS; or, Rambles and Incidents in search of Alpine Plants. Crown 8vo. cloth. 6s.

The aim of this book is to impart a general idea of the origin, character, and distribution of those rare and beautiful Alpine plants which occur on the British hills, and which are found almost everywhere on the lofty mountain chains of Europe, Asia, Africa, and America. The information the author has to give is conveyed in untechnical language, in a setting of personal adventure, and associated with descriptions of the natural scenery and the peculiarities of the human life in the midst of which the plants were found. By this method the subject is made interesting to a very large class of readers. "Botanical knowledge is blended with a love of nature, a pious enthusiasm, and a rich felicity of diction not to be met with in any works of kindred character, if we except those of Hugh Miller."—TELEGRAPH. *"Mr. M.'s glowing pictures of Scandinavian scenery."*—SATURDAY REVIEW.

Martin (Frederick).—THE STATESMAN'S YEAR-BOOK :
See p. 36 of this Catalogue.

Martineau.—BIOGRAPHICAL SKETCHES, 1852—1868. By HARRIET MARTINEAU. Third and Cheaper Edition, with New Preface. Crown 8vo. 6s.

A Collection of Memoirs under these several sections:—(1) *Royal*, (2) *Politicians*, (3) *Professional*, (4) *Scientific*, (5) *Social*, (6) *Literary. These Memoirs appeared originally in the columns of the* DAILY NEWS. *"Miss Martineau's large literary powers and her fine intellectual training make these little sketches more instructive, and constitute them more genuinely works of art, than many more ambitious and diffuse biographies."*—FORTNIGHTLY REVIEW. *"Each memoir is a complete digest of a celebrated life, illuminated by the flood of searching light which streams from the gaze of an acute but liberal mind."*—MORNING STAR.

Masson (David).—For other Works by same Author, *see* PHILOSOPHICAL and BELLES LETTRES CATALOGUES.

LIFE OF JOHN MILTON. Narrated in connection with the Political, Ecclesiastical, and Literary History of his Time. By DAVID MASSON, M.A., LL.D., Professor of Rhetoric and English Literature in the University of Edinburgh. Vol. I. with Portraits. 8vo. 18s. Vol. II., 1638—1643. 8vo. 16s. Vol. III. in the press.

This work is not only a Biography, but also a continuous Political, Ecclesiastical, and Literary History of England through Milton's whole time. In order to understand Milton, his position, his motives, his thoughts by himself, his public words to his countrymen, and the probable effect of those words, it was necessary to refer largely to the History of his Time, not only as it is presented in well-known books, but as it had to be rediscovered by express and laborious investigation in original and forgotten records: thus of the Biography, a History grew: not a mere popular compilation, but a work of independent search and method from first to last, which has cost more labour by far than the Biography. The second volume is so arranged that the reader may select or omit either the History or Biography. The NORTH BRITISH REVIEW, *speaking of the first volume of this work said,* " *The Life of Milton is here written once for all.*" *The* NONCONFORMIST, *in noticing the second volume, says,* " *Its literary excellence entitles it to take its place in the first ranks of our literature, while the whole style of its execution marks it as the only book that has done anything like adequate justice to one of the great masters of our language, and one of our truest patriots, as well as our greatest epic poet.*"

Mayor (J. E. B.)—WORKS Edited By JOHN E. B. MAYOR, M.A., Fellow of St. John's College, Cambridge.

CAMBRIDGE IN THE SEVENTEENTH CENTURY. Part II. Autobiography of Matthew Robinson. Fcap. 8vo. 5s. 6d.

This is the second of the Memoirs illustrative of " *Cambridge in the Seventeenth Century,*" *that of Nicholas Farrar having preceded it. It gives a lively picture of England during the Civil Wars, the most important crisis of our national life; it supplies materials for the history of the University and our Endowed Schools, and gives us a view of country clergy at a time when they are supposed to have been, with scarce an exception, scurrilous sots. Mr. Mayor has added a collection of extracts and documents relating to the history of several other Cambridge men of note belonging to the same period, all, like Robinson, of Nonconformist leanings.*

LIFE OF BISHOP BEDELL. By his SON. Fcap. 8vo. 3s. 6d.

This is the third of the Memoirs illustrative of " *Cambridge in the 17th Century.*" *The life of the Bishop of Kilmore here printed for the first time is preserved in the Tanner MSS., and is preliminary to a larger one to be issued shortly.*

Mitford (A. B.)—TALES OF OLD JAPAN. By A. B. MITFORD, Second Secretary to the British Legation in Japan. With upwards of 30 Illustrations, drawn and cut on Wood by Japanese Artists. Two Vols. crown 8vo. 21s.

Under the influence of more enlightened ideas and of a liberal system of policy, the old Japanese civilization is fast disappearing, and will, in a few years, be completely extinct. It was important, therefore, to preserve as far as possible trustworthy records of a state of society which, although venerable from its antiquity, has for Europeans the dawn of novelty; hence the series of narratives and legends translated by Mr. Mitford, and in which the Japanese are very judiciously left to tell their own tale. The two volumes comprise not only stories and episodes illustrative of Asiatic superstitions, but also three sermons. The preface, appendices, and notes explain a number of local peculiarities; the thirty-one woodcuts are the genuine work of a native artist, who, unconsciously of course, has adopted the process first introduced by the early German masters. "These very original volumes will always be interesting as memorials of a most exceptional society, while regarded simply as tales, they are sparkling, sensational, and dramatic, and the originality of their ideas and the quaintness of their language give them a most captivating piquancy. The illustrations are extremely interesting, and for the curious in such matters have a special and particular value."—PALL MALL GAZETTE.

Morley (John).—EDMUND BURKE, a Historical Study. By JOHN MORLEY, B.A. Oxon. Crown 8vo. 7s. 6d.

"The style is terse and incisive, and brilliant with epigram and point. It contains pithy aphoristic sentences which Burke himself would not have disowned. Its sustained power of reasoning, its wide sweep of observation and reflection, its elevated ethical and social tone, stamp it as a work of high excellence."—SATURDAY REVIEW. "A model of compact condensation. We have seldom met with a book in which so much matter was compressed into so limited a space."—PALL MALL GAZETTE. "An essay of unusual effort."—WESTMINSTER REVIEW.

Morison.—THE LIFE AND TIMES OF SAINT BERNARD, Abbot of Clairvaux. By JAMES COTTER MORISON, M.A. Cheaper Edition. Crown 8vo. 4s. 6d.

The PALL MALL GAZETTE calls this "one of the best contributions in our literature towards a vivid, intelligent, and worthy knowledge of European interests and thoughts and feelings during the twelfth century. A delightful and instructive volume, and one of the best products of the modern historic spirit." "A work," says the NONCONFORMIST, "of great merit and value, dealing most thoroughly with one of the most interesting characters, and one of the most interesting periods, in the Church history of the Middle Ages. Mr. Morison is thoroughly master of his subject, *and writes with great discrimination and fairness, and in a chaste and elegant style."* The SPECTATOR *says it is "not only distinguished by research and candour, it has also the great merit of never being dull."*

Palgrave (Sir F.)—HISTORY OF NORMANDY AND OF ENGLAND. By Sir FRANCIS PALGRAVE, Deputy Keeper of Her Majesty's Public Records. Completing the History to the Death of William Rufus. Four Vols. 8vo. £4 4s.

Volume I. General Relations of Mediæval Europe—The Carlovingian Empire—The Danish Expeditions in the Gauls—And the Establishment of Rollo. Volume II. The Three First Dukes of Normandy; Rollo, Guillaume Longue-Épée, and Richard Sans-Peur—The Carlovingian line supplanted by the Capets. Volume III. Richard Sans-Peur—Richard Le-Bon—Richard III.—Robert Le Diable—William the Conqueror. Volume IV. William Rufus—Accession of Henry Beauclerc. It is needless to say anything to recommend this work of a lifetime to all students of history; it is, as the SPECTATOR *says, "perhaps the greatest single contribution yet made to the authentic annals of this country," and "must," says the* NONCONFORMIST, *"always rank among our standard authorities."*

Palgrave (W. G.)—A NARRATIVE OF A YEAR'S JOURNEY THROUGH CENTRAL AND EASTERN ARABIA, 1862-3. By LIAM GIFFORD PALGRAVE, late of the Eighth Regiment Bombay N. I. Sixth Edition. With Maps, Plans, and Portrait of Author, engraved on steel by Jeens. Crown 8vo. 6s.

*"The work is a model of what its class should be; the style restrained, the narrative clear, telling us all we wish to know of the country and people visited, and enough of the author and his feelings to enable us to trust ourselves to his guidance in a tract hitherto untrodden, and dangerous in more senses than one. . . He has not only written one of the best books on the Arabs and one of the best books on Arabia, but he has done so in a manner that must command the respect no less than the admiration of his fellow-countrymen."—*FORTNIGHTLY REVIEW. *" Considering the extent of our previous ignorance, the amount of his achievements, and the importance of his contributions to our knowledge, we cannot say less of him than was once said of a far greater discoverer—Mr. Palgrave has indeed given a new world to Europe."—*PALL MALL GAZETTE.

HISTORY, BIOGRAPHY, & TRAVELS.

Paris.—INSIDE PARIS DURING THE SIEGE. By an OXFORD GRADUATE. Crown 8vo. 7s. 6d.

This volume consists of the diary kept by a gentleman who lived in Paris during the whole of its siege by the Prussians. He had many facilities for coming in contact with men of all parties and of all classes, and ascertaining the actual motives which animated them, and their real ultimate aims. These facilities he took advantage of, and in his diary, day by day, carefully recorded the results of his observations, as well as faithfully but graphically photographed the various incidents of the siege which came under his own notice, the actual condition of the besieged, the sayings and doings, the hopes and fears of the people among whom he freely moved. In the Appendix is an exhaustive and elaborate account of the Organization of the Republican party, sent to the author by M. Jules Andrieu; and a translation of the Manifesto of the Commune to the People of England, dated April 19, 1871. "*The author tells his story admirably. The Oxford Graduate seems to have gone everywhere, heard what everyone had to say, and so been able to give us photographs of Paris life during the siege which we have not had from any other source.*"—SPECTATOR. "*He has written brightly, lightly, and pleasantly, yet in perfect good taste.*"—SATURDAY REVIEW.

Prichard.—THE ADMINISTRATION OF INDIA. From 1859 to 1868. The First Ten Years of Administration under the Crown. By ILTUDUS THOMAS PRICHARD, Barrister-at-Law. Two Vols. Demy 8vo. With Map. 21s.

In these volumes the author has aimed to supply a full, impartial, and independent account of British India between 1859 and 1868—which is in many respects the most important epoch in the history of that country that the present century has seen. "*It has the great merit that it is not exclusively devoted, as are too many histories, to military and political details, but enters thoroughly into the more important questions of social history. We find in these volumes a well-arranged and compendious reference to almost all that has been done in India during the last ten years; and the most important official documents and historical pieces are well selected and duly set forth.*"—SCOTSMAN. "*It is a work which every Englishman in India ought to add to his library.*"—STAR OF INDIA.

Robinson (H. Crabb)—THE DIARY, REMINISCENCES, AND CORRESPONDENCE, OF HENRY CRABB ROBINSON, Barrister-at-Law. Selected and Edited by THOMAS SADLER, Ph.D. With Portrait. Third and Cheaper Edition. Two Vols. Crown 8vo. 16s.

The DAILY NEWS *says: " The two books which are most likely to survive change of literary taste, and to charm while instructing generation after generation, are the 'Diary' of Pepys and Boswell's 'Life of Johnson.' The day will come when to these many will add the 'Diary of Henry Crabb Robinson.' Excellences like those which render the personal revelations of Pepys and the observations of Boswell such pleasant reading abound in this work . . . . In it is to be found something to suit every taste and inform every mind. For the general reader it contains much light and amusing matter. To the lover of literature it conveys information which he will prize highly on account of its accuracy and rarity. The student of social life will gather from it many valuable hints whereon to base theories as to the effects on English society of the progress of civilization. For these and other reasons this 'Diary' is a work to which a hearty welcome should be accorded."*

Rogers (James E. Thorold).—HISTORICAL GLEANINGS : A Series of Sketches. Montague, Walpole, Adam Smith, Cobbett. By Prof. ROGERS. Crown 8vo. 4s. 6d. Second Series. Wiklif, Laud, Wilkes, and Horne Tooke. Crown 8vo. 6s.

Professor Rogers's object in these sketches, which are in the form of Lectures, is to present a set of historical facts, grouped round a principal figure. The author has aimed to state the social facts of the time in which the individual whose history is handled took part in public business. It is from sketches like these of the great men who took a prominent and influential part in the affairs of their time that a clear conception of the social and economical condition of our ancestors can be obtained. History learned in this way is both instructive and agreeable. " His Essays," the PALL MALL GAZETTE *says, " are full of interest, pregnant, thoughtful, and readable." " They rank far above the average of similar performances," says the* WESTMINSTER REVIEW.

Raphael.—RAPHAEL OF URBINO AND HIS FATHER GIOVANNI SANTI. By J. D. PASSAVANT, formerly Director of the Museum at Frankfort. With Twenty Permanent Photographs. Royal 8vo. Handsomely bound. 31s. 6d.

To the enlarged French edition of Passavant's *Life of Raphael*, that painter's admirers have turned whenever they have sought information, and it will doubtless remain for many years the best book of reference on all questions pertaining to the great painter. The present work consists of a translation of those parts of Passavant's volumes which are most likely to interest the general reader. Besides a complete life of Raphael, it contains the valuable descriptions of all his known paintings, and the Chronological Index, which is of so much service to amateurs who wish to study the progressive character of his works. The Illustrations by Woodbury's new permanent process of photography, are taken from the finest engravings that could be procured, and have been chosen with the intention of giving examples of Raphael's various styles of painting. The SATURDAY REVIEW says of them, "We have seen not a few elegant specimens of Mr. Woodbury's new process, but we have seen none that equal these."

Sadler.—EDWIN WILKINS FIELD. A Memorial Sketch. By THOMAS SADLER, Ph. D. With a Portrait. Crown 8vo. 4s. 6d.

Mr. Field was well known during his life-time not only as an eminent lawyer and a strenuous and successful advocate of law reform, but, both in England and America, as a man of wide and thorough culture, varied tastes, large-heartedness, and lofty aims. His sudden death was looked upon as a public loss, and it is expected that this brief Memoir will be acceptable to a large number outside of the many friends at whose request it has been written.

Somers (Robert).—THE SOUTHERN STATES SINCE THE WAR. By ROBERT SOMERS. With Map. 8vo. 9s.

This work is the result of inquiries made by the author of all authorities competent to afford him information, and of his own observation during a lengthened sojourn in the Southern States, to which writers on America so seldom direct their steps. The author's object is to give some account of the condition of the Southern States under the new social and political system introduced by the civil war. He has here collected such notes of the progress of their cotton plantations, of the state of their labouring population and of their industrial enterprises, as may help the reader to a safe opinion of their means and prospects of development. He also gives such information of their natural resources, railways, and other public works, as may tend to show to what extent they are fitted to become a profitable field of enlarged immigration, settlement, and foreign trade. The volume contains many valuable and reliable details as to the condition of the Negro population, the state of Education and Religion, of Cotton, Sugar, and Tobacco Cultivation, of Agriculture generally, of Coal and Iron Mining, Manufactures, Trade, Means of Locomotion, and the condition of Towns and of Society. A large map of the Southern States by Messrs. W. and A. K. Johnston is appended, which shows with great clearness the Cotton, Coal, and Iron districts, the railways completed and projected, the State boundaries, and other important details. "Full of interesting and valuable information."—SATURDAY REVIEW.

Smith (Professor Goldwin).—THREE ENGLISH STATESMEN. See p. 37 of this Catalogue.

Streets and Lanes of a City.—See DUTTON (AMY) p. 31 of this Catalogue.

Tacitus.—THE HISTORY OF TACITUS, translated into English. By A. J. CHURCH, M.A. and W. J. BRODRIBB, M.A. With a Map and Notes. 8vo. 10s. 6d.

The translators have endeavoured to adhere as closely to the original as was thought consistent with a proper observance of English idiom. At the same time it has been their aim to reproduce the precise expressions of the author. This work is characterised by the SPECTATOR as "a scholarly and faithful translation."

THE AGRICOLA AND GERMANIA. Translated into English by A. J. CHURCH, M.A. and W. J. BRODRIBB, M.A. With Maps and Notes. Extra fcap. 8vo. 2s. 6d.

The translators have sought to produce such a version as may satisfy scholars who demand a faithful rendering of the original, and English readers who are offended by the baldness and frigidity which commonly disfigure translations. The treatises are accompanied by Introductions, Notes, Maps, and a chronological Summary. The ATHENÆUM says of this work that it is "a version at once readable and exact, which may be perused with pleasure by all, and consulted with advantage by the classical student;" and the PALL MALL GAZETTE says, "What the editors have attempted to do, it is not, we think probable that any living scholars could have done better."

Taylor (Rev. Isaac).—WORDS AND PLACES. *See* p. 44 of this Catalogue.

Trench (Archbishop).—For other Works by the same Author, *see* THEOLOGICAL and BELLES LETTRES CATALOGUES, and p. 45 of this Catalogue.

GUSTAVUS ADOLPHUS: Social Aspects of the Thirty Years, War. By R. CHENEVIX TRENCH, D.D., Archbishop of Dublin. Fcap. 8vo. 2s. 6d.

" Clear and lucid in style, these lectures will be a treasure to many to whom the subject is unfamiliar."—DUBLIN EVENING MAIL. *" These Lectures are vivid and graphic sketches: the first treats of the great King of Sweden, and of his character rather than of his actions; the second describes the condition of Germany in that dreadful time when famine, battles, and pestilence, though they exterminated three-fourths of the population, were less terrible than the fiend-like cruelty, the utter lawlessness and depravity, bred of long anarchy and suffering. The substance of the lectures is drawn from contemporary accounts, which give to them especial freshness and life."*—LITERARY CHURCHMAN.

Trench (Mrs. R.)—Remains of the late MRS. RICHARD TRENCH. Being Selections from her Journals, Letters, and other Papers. Edited by ARCHBISHOP TRENCH. New and Cheaper Issue, with Portrait. 8vo. 6s.

Contains Notices and Anecdotes illustrating the social life of the period —extending over a quarter of a century (1799—1827). It includes also Poems and other miscellaneous pieces by Mrs. Trench.

Wallace.—Works by ALFRED RUSSEL WALLACE. For other Works by same Author, *see* SCIENTIFIC CATALOGUE.

Dr. Hooker, in his address to the British Association, spoke thus of the author:—" Of Mr. Wallace and his many contributions to philosophical biology it is not easy to speak without enthusiasm ; for, putting aside their great merits, he, throughout his writings, with a modesty as rare as I believe it to be unconscious, forgets his own unquestioned claim to the honour of having originated, independently of Mr. Darwin, the theories which he so ably defends."

Wallace (A. R.)—*continued.*

A NARRATIVE OF TRAVELS ON THE AMAZON AND RIO NEGRO, with an Account of the Native Tribes, and Observations on the Climate, Geology, and Natural History of the Amazon Valley. With a Map and Illustrations. 8vo. 12s.

Mr. Wallace is acknowledged as one of the first of modern travellers and naturalists. This, his earliest work, will be found to possess many charms for the general reader, and to be full of interest to the student of natural history.

THE MALAY ARCHIPELAGO: the Land of the Orang Utan and the Bird of Paradise. A Narrative of Travel with Studies of Man and Nature. With Maps and Illustrations. Third and Cheaper Edition. Crown 8vo. 7s. 6d.

"*The result is a vivid picture of tropical life, which may be read with unflagging interest, and a sufficient account of his scientific conclusions to stimulate our appetite without wearying us by detail. In short, we may safely say that we have never read a more agreeable book of its kind.*"— SATURDAY REVIEW. "*His descriptions of scenery, of the people and their manners and customs, enlivened by occasional amusing anecdotes, constitute the most interesting reading we have taken up for some time.*"— STANDARD.

Ward (Professor).—THE HOUSE OF AUSTRIA IN THE THIRTY YEARS' WAR. Two Lectures, with Notes and Illustrations. By ADOLPHUS W. WARD, M.A., Professor of History in Owens College, Manchester. Extra fcap. 8vo. 2s. 6d.

These two Lectures were delivered in February, 1869, at the Philosophical Institution, Edinburgh, and are now published with Notes and Illustrations. bear more thoroughly the impress of one who has a true and vigorous grasp "*We have never read,*" *says the* SATURDAY REVIEW, "*any lectures which of the subject in hand.*" "*They are,*" *the* SCOTSMAN *says,* "*the fruit of much labour and learning, and it would be difficult to compress into a hundred pages more information.*"

Warren.—AN ESSAY ON GREEK FEDERAL COINAGE. By the Hon. J. LEICESTER WARREN, M.A. 8vo. 2s. 6d.

The present essay is an attempt to illustrate Mr. Freeman's Federal Government by evidence deduced from the coinage of the times and countries therein treated of.

Wedgwood.—JOHN WESLEY AND THE EVANGELICAL REACTION of the Eighteenth Century. By JULIA WEDGWOOD. Crown 8vo. 8s. 6d.

This book is an attempt to delineate the influence of a particular man upon his age. The background to the central figure is treated with considerable minuteness, the object of representation being not the vicissitude of a particular life, but that element in the life which impressed itself on the life of a nation,—an element which cannot be understood without a study of aspects of national thought which on a superficial view might appear wholly unconnected with it. "*In style and intellectual power, in breadth of view and clearness of insight, Miss Wedgwood's book far surpasses all rivals.*"—ATHENÆUM. "*As a short account of the most remarkable movement in the eighteenth century, it must fairly be described as excellent.*"—PALL MALL GAZETTE.

Wilson.—A MEMOIR OF GEORGE WILSON, M.D., F.R.S.E., Regius Professor of Technology in the University of Edinburgh. By his SISTER. New Edition. Crown 8vo. 6s.

"*An exquisite and touching portrait of a rare and beautiful spirit.*"— GUARDIAN. "*He more than most men of whom we have lately read deserved a minute and careful biography, and by such alone could he be understood, and become loveable and influential to his fellow-men. Such a biography his sister has written, in which letters reach almost to the extent of a complete autobiography, with all the additional charm of being unconsciously such. We revere and admire the heart, and earnestly praise the patient tender hand, by which such a worthy record of the earth-story of one of God's true angel-men has been constructed for our delight and profit.*"—NONCONFORMIST.

Wilson (Daniel, LL.D.)—Works by DANIEL WILSON, LL.D., Professor of History and English Literature in University College, Toronto :—

PREHISTORIC ANNALS OF SCOTLAND. New Edition, with numerous Illustrations. Two Vols. demy 8vo. 36s.

One object aimed at when the book first appeared was to rescue archæological research from that limited range to which a too exclusive devotion to classical studies had given rise, and, especially in relation to Scotland, to prove how greatly more comprehensive and important are its native antiquities than all

Wilson (Daniel, LL.D.)—*continued.*

the traces of intruded art. The aim has been to a large extent effectually accomplished, and such an impulse given to archæological research, that in this new edition the whole of the work has had to be remodelled. Fully a third of it has been entirely re-written; and the remaining portions have undergone so minute a revision as to render it in many respects a new work. The number of pictorial illustrations has been greatly increased, and several of the former plates and woodcuts have been re-engraved from new drawings. This is divided into four Parts. Part *I.* deals with The Primeval or Stone Period: *Aboriginal Traces, Sepulchral Memorials, Dwellings, and Catacombs, Temples, Weapons, etc. etc.;* Part *II.* The Bronze Period: *The Metallurgic Transition, Primitive Bronze, Personal Ornaments, Religion, Arts, and Domestic Habits,* with other topics; *Part III.* The Iron Period: *The Introduction of Iron, The Roman Invasion, Strongholds, etc. etc.; Part IV.* The Christian Period: *Historical Data, the Norrie's Law Relics, Primitive and Mediæval Ecclesiology, Ecclesiastical and Miscellaneous Antiquities. The work is furnished with an elaborate Index.* "*One of the most interesting, learned, and elegant works we have seen for a long time.*"—WESTMINSTER REVIEW. "*The interest connected with this beautiful volume is not limited to that part of the kingdom to which it is chiefly devoted; it will be consulted with advantage and gratification by all who have a regard for National Antiquities and for the advancement of scientific Archæology.*"— ARCHÆOLOGICAL JOURNAL.

PREHISTORIC MAN. New Edition, revised and partly re-written, with numerous Illustrations. One vol. 8vo. 21*s.*

This work, which carries out the principle of the preceding one, but with a wider scope, aims to "*view Man, as far as possible, unaffected by those modifying influences which accompany the development of nations and the maturity of a true historic period, in order thereby to ascertain the sources from whence such development and maturity proceed. These researches into the origin of civilization have accordingly been pursued under the belief which influenced the author in previous inquiries that the investigations of the archæologist, when carried on in an enlightened spirit, are replete with interest in relation to some of the most important problems of modern science. To reject the aid of archæology in the progress of science, and especially of ethnological science, is to extinguish the lamp of the student when most dependent on its borrowed rays.*" *A prolonged residence on some of the newest sites of the New World has afforded the author many*

Wilson (Daniel, LL.D.)—*continued.*

opportunities of investigating the antiquities of the American Aborigines, and of bringing to light many facts of high importance in reference to primeval man. The changes in the new edition, necessitated by the great advance in Archæology since the first, include both reconstruction and condensation, along with considerable additions alike in illustration and in argument. " *We find,*" *says the* ATHENÆUM, " *the main idea of his treatise to be a pre-eminently scientific one,—namely, by archæological records to obtain a definite conception of the origin and nature of man's earliest efforts at civilization in the New World, and to endeavour to discover, as if by analogy, the necessary conditions, phases, and epochs through which man in the prehistoric stage in the Old World also must necessarily have passed.*" *The* NORTH BRITISH REVIEW *calls it* " *a mature and mellow work of an able man; free alike from crotchets and from dogmatism, and exhibiting on every page the caution and moderation of a well-balanced judgment.*"

CHATTERTON: A Biographical Study. By DANIEL WILSON, LL.D., Professor of History and English Literature in University College, Toronto. Crown 8vo. 6s. 6d.

The author here regards Chatterton as a poet, not as a " *mere resetter and defacer of stolen literary treasures.*" *Reviewed in this light, he has found much in the old materials capable of being turned to new account; and to these materials research in various directions has enabled him to make some additions. He believes that the boy-poet has been misjudged, and that the biographies hitherto written of him are not only imperfect but untrue. While dealing tenderly, the author has sought to deal truthfully with the failings as well as the virtues of the boy: bearing always in remembrance, what has been too frequently lost sight of, that he was but a boy;—a boy, and yet a poet of rare power. The* EXAMINER *thinks this* " *the most complete and the purest biography of the poet which has yet appeared.*" *The* LITERARY CHURCHMAN *calls it* " *a most charming literary biography.*"

Yonge (Charlotte M.)—Works by CHARLOTTE M. YONGE, Author of "The Heir of Redclyffe," &c. &c. :—

A PARALLEL HISTORY OF FRANCE AND ENGLAND: consisting of Outlines and Dates. Oblong 4to. 3s. 6d.

This tabular history has been drawn up to supply a want felt by many teachers of some means of making their pupils realize what events in the

Yonge (Charlotte M.)—*continued*.

two countries were contemporary. A skeleton narrative has been constructed of the chief transactions in either country, placing a column between for what affected both alike, by which means it is hoped that young people may be assisted in grasping the mutual relation of events.

CAMEOS FROM ENGLISH HISTORY. From Rollo to Edward II. Extra fcap. 8vo. Second Edition, enlarged. 5s.

A SECOND SERIES, THE WARS IN FRANCE. Extra fcap. 8vo. 5s.

The endeavour has not been to chronicle facts, but to put together a series of pictures of persons and events, so as to arrest the attention, and give some individuality and distinctness to the recollection, by gathering together details of the most memorable moments. The "Cameos" are intended as a book for young people just beyond the elementary histories of England, and able to enter in some degree into the real spirit of events, and to be struck with characters and scenes presented in some relief. "Instead of dry details," says the NONCONFORMIST,*" we have living pictures, faithful, vivid, and striking."*

Young (Julian Charles, M.A.)—A MEMOIR OF CHARLES MAYNE YOUNG, Tragedian, with Extracts from his Son's Journal. By JULIAN CHARLES YOUNG, M.A. Rector of Ilmington. With Portraits and Sketches. *New and Cheaper Edition.* Crown 8vo. 7s. 6d.

Round this memoir of one who held no mean place in public estimation as a tragedian, and who, as a man, by the unobtrusive simplicity and moral purity of his private life, won golden opinions from all sorts of men, are clustered extracts from the author's Journals, containing many curious and interesting reminiscences of his father's and his own eminent and famous contemporaries and acquaintances, somewhat after the manner of H. Crabb Robinson's Diary. Every page will be found full both of entertainment and instruction. It contains four portraits of the tragedian, and a few other curious sketches. "In this budget of anecdotes, fables, and gossip, old and new, relative to Scott, Moore, Chalmers, Coleridge, Wordsworth, Croker, Mathews, the third and fourth Georges, Bowles, Beckford, Lockhart, Wellington, Peel, Louis Napoleon, D'Orsay, Dickens, Thackeray, Louis Blanc, Gibson, Constable, and Stanfield, etc. etc. the reader must be hard indeed to please who cannot find entertainment."— PALL MALL GAZETTE.

POLITICS, POLITICAL AND SOCIAL ECONOMY, LAW, AND KINDRED SUBJECTS.

Baxter.—NATIONAL INCOME: The United Kingdom. By R. DUDLEY BAXTER, M.A. 8vo. 3s. 6d.

The present work endeavours to answer systematically such questions as the following:—What are the means and aggregate wages of our labouring population; what are the numbers and aggregate profits of the middle classes; what the revenues of our great proprietors and capitalists; and what the pecuniary strength of the nation to bear the burdens annually falling upon us? What capital in land and goods and money is stored up for our subsistence, and for carrying out our enterprises? The author has collected his facts from every quarter and tested them in various ways, in order to make his statements and deductions valuable and trustworthy. Part I. of the work deals with the Classification of the Population into—*Chap. I.* The Income Classes; *Chap. II.* The Upper and Middle and Manual Labour Classes. *Part II. treats of the* Income of the United Kingdom, *divided into—Chap. III.* Upper and Middle Incomes; *Chap. IV.* Wages of the Manual Labour Classes—England and Wales; *Chap. V.* Income of Scotland; *Chap. VI.* Income of Ireland; *Chap. VII.* Income of the United Kingdom. *In the Appendix will be found many valuable and carefully compiled tables, illustrating in detail the subjects discussed in the text.*

Bernard.—FOUR LECTURES ON SUBJECTS CONNECTED WITH DIPLOMACY. By MOUNTAGUE BERNARD, M.A., Chichele Professor of International Law and Diplomacy, Oxford. 8vo. 9s.

These four Lectures deal with—I. "The Congress of Westphalia;" II. "Systems of Policy;" III. "Diplomacy, Past and Present;" IV. "The Obligations of Treaties."—"*Singularly interesting lectures, so able, clear, and attractive.*"—SPECTATOR. "*The author of these lectures is full of the knowledge which belongs to his subject, and has that power of clear and vigorous expression which results from clear and vigorous thought.*"—SCOTSMAN.

Bright (John, M.P.)—SPEECHES ON QUESTIONS OF PUBLIC POLICY. By the Right Hon. JOHN BRIGHT, M.P. Edited by Professor THOROLD ROGERS. Author's Popular Edition. Globe 8vo. 3s. 6d.

The speeches which have been selected for publication in these volumes possess a value, as examples of the art of public speaking, which no person will be likely to underrate. The speeches have been selected with a view of supplying the public with the evidence on which Mr. Bright's friends assert his right to a place in the front rank of English statesmen. They are divided into groups, according to their subjects. The editor has naturally given prominence to those subjects with which Mr. Bright has been specially identified, as, for example, India, America, Ireland, and Parliamentary Reform. But nearly every topic of great public interest on which Mr. Bright has spoken is represented in these volumes. "Mr. Bright's speeches will always deserve to be studied, as an apprenticeship to popular and parliamentary oratory; they will form materials for the history of our time, and many brilliant passages, perhaps some entire speeches, will really become a part of the living literature of England."—DAILY NEWS.

LIBRARY EDITION. Two Vols. 8vo. With Portrait. 25s.

Christie.—THE BALLOT AND CORRUPTION AND EXPENDITURE AT ELECTIONS, a Collection of Essays and Addresses of different dates. By W. D. CHRISTIE, C.B., formerly Her Majesty's Minister to the Argentine Confederation and to Brazil; Author of "Life of the First Earl of Shaftesbury." Crown 8vo. 4s. 6d.

Mr. Christie has been well known for upwards of thirty years as a strenuous and able advocate for the Ballot, both in his place in Parliament and elsewhere. The papers and speeches here collected are six in number, exclusive of the Preface and Dedication to Professor Maurice, which contains many interesting historical details concerning the Ballot. "You have thought to greater purpose on the means of preventing electoral corruption, and are likely to be of more service in passing measures for that highly important end, than any other person that I could name."—J. S. Mill, in a published letter to the Author, May 1868.

Corfield (Professor W. H.)—A DIGEST OF FACTS RELATING TO THE TREATMENT AND UTILIZATION OF SEWAGE. By W. H. CORFIELD, M.A., B.A., Professor of Hygiene and Public Health at University College, London. 8vo. 10s. 6d. Second Edition, corrected and enlarged.

*In this edition the author has revised and corrected the entire work, and made many important additions. The headings of the eleven chapters are as follow:—I. "Early Systems: Midden-Heaps and Cesspools." II. "Filth and Disease—Cause and Effect." III. "Improved Midden-Pits and Cesspools; Midden-Closets, Pail-Closets, etc." IV. "The Dry-Closet Systems." V. "Water-Closets." VI. "Sewerage." VII. "Sanitary Aspects of the Water-Carrying System." VIII. "Value of Sewage; Injury to Rivers." IX. Town Sewage; Attempts at Utilization." X. "Filtration and Irrigation." XI. "Influence of Sewage Farming on the Public Health." An abridged account of the more recently published researches on the subject will be found in the Appendices, while the Summary contains a concise statement of the views which the author himself has been led to adopt; references have been inserted throughout to show from what sources the numerous quotations have been derived, and an Index has been added. "Mr. Corfield's work is entitled to rank as a standard authority, no less than a convenient handbook, in all matters relating to sewage."—*ATHENÆUM.

Dutton (Amy).—STREETS AND LANES OF A CITY: being the Reminiscences of AMY DUTTON. With a Preface by the BISHOP OF SALISBURY. Pp. viii. 159. Globe 8vo. 3s. 6d.

This little volume records "a portion of the experience, selected out of overflowing materials, of two ladies, during several years of devoted work as district parochial visitors in a large population in the North of England." The "Reminiscences of Amy Dutton" serve *to illustrate the line of argument adopted by Miss Stephen in her work on the "Service of the Poor," because they show that as in one aspect the lady visitor may be said to be a link between rich and poor, in another she helps to blend the "religious" life with the "secular," and in both does service of extreme value to the Church and Nation. "A record only too brief of some of the real portraits of humanity, painted by a pencil, tender indeed and sympathetic, but with too clear a sight, too ready a sense of humour, and too conscientious a spirit ever to exaggerate, extenuate, or aught set down in malice."—*GUARDIAN.

Fawcett.—Works by HENRY FAWCETT, M.A., M.P., Fellow of Trinity Hall, and Professor of Political Economy in the University of Cambridge :—

THE ECONOMIC POSITION OF THE BRITISH LABOURER. Extra fcap. 8vo. 5s.

This work formed a portion of a course of Lectures delivered by the author in the University of Cambridge, and he has deemed it advisable to retain many of the expositions of the elementary principles of Economic Science. In the Introductory Chapter the author points out the scope of the work and shows the vast importance of the subject in relation to the commercial prosperity and even the national existence of Britain. Then follow five chapters on "The Land Tenure of England," "Co-operation," "The Causes which regulate Wages," "Trade Unions and Strikes," and "Emigration." The EXAMINER *calls the work "a very scholarly exposition on some of the most essential questions of Political Economy;" and the* NONCONFORMIST *says "it is written with charming freshness, ease, and lucidity."*

MANUAL OF POLITICAL ECONOMY. Third and Cheaper Edition, with Two New Chapters. Crown 8vo. 10s. 6d.

In this treatise no important branch of the subject has been omitted, and the author believes that the principles which are therein explained will enable the reader to obtain a tolerably complete view of the whole science. Mr. Fawcett has endeavoured to show how intimately Political Economy is connected with the practical questions of life. For the convenience of the ordinary reader, and especially for those who may use the book to prepare themselves for

Fawcett (H.)—*continued.*

examinations, he has prefixed a very detailed summary of Contents, which may be regarded as an analysis of the work. The new edition has been so carefully revised that there is scarcely a page in which some improvement has not been introduced. The DAILY NEWS *says:* "*It forms one of the best introductions to the principles of the science, and to its practical applications in the problems of modern, and especially of English, government and society.*" "*The book is written throughout,*" says the EXAMINER. "*with admirable force, clearness, and brevity, every important part of the subject being duly considered.*"

PAUPERISM : ITS CAUSES AND REMEDIES. Crown 8vo. 5*s.* 6*d.*

In its number for March 11th, 1871, the SPECTATOR *said:* "*We wish Professor Fawcett would devote a little more of his time and energy to the practical consideration of that monster problem of Pauperism, for the treatment of which his economic knowledge and popular sympathies so eminently fit him.*" *The volume now published may be regarded as an answer to the above challenge. The seven chapters it comprises discuss the following subjects:—I. "Pauperism and the old Poor Law." II. "The present Poor Law System." III. "The Increase of Population." IV. "National Education : its Economic and Social Effects." V. "Co-partnership and Co-operation." VI. "The English System of Land Tenure." VII. "The Inclosure of Commons." The* ATHENÆUM *calls the work* "*a repertory of interesting and well-digested information.*"

ESSAYS ON POLITICAL AND SOCIAL SUBJECTS. By PROFESSOR FAWCETT, M.P., and MILLICENT GARRETT FAWCETT. 8vo. 10*s.* 6*d.*

This volume contains fourteen papers, some of which have appeared in various journals and periodicals ; others have not before been published. They are all on subjects of great importance and universal interest, and the names of the two authors are a sufficient guarantee that each topic is discussed with full knowledge, great ability, clearness, and earnestness. The following are some of the titles:—"*Modern Socialism ;*" "*Free Education in its Economic Aspects ;*" "*Pauperism, Charity, and the Poor Law ;*" "*National Debt and National Prosperity ;*" "*What can be done for the*

Agricultural Labourers ;" " The Education of Women ;" " The Electoral Disabilities of Women ;" " The House of Lords." Each article is signed with the initials of its author.

Fawcett (Mrs.)—POLITICAL ECONOMY FOR BEGINNERS. WITH QUESTIONS. By MILLICENT GARRETT FAWCETT. 18mo. 2s. 6d.

In this little work are explained as briefly as possible the most important principles of Political Economy, in the hope that it will be useful to beginners, and perhaps be an assistance to those who are desirous of introducing the study of Political Economy to schools. In order to adapt the book especially for school use, questions have been added at the end of each chapter. The DAILY NEWS *calls it "clear, compact, and comprehensive;" and the* SPECTATOR *says, "Mrs. Fawcett's treatise is perfectly suited to its purpose."*

Freeman (E. A., M.A., D.C.L.)—HISTORY OF FEDERAL GOVERNMENT. See p. 6 of preceding HISTORICAL CATALOGUE.

Godkin (James).—THE LAND WAR IN IRELAND. A History for the Times. By JAMES GODKIN, Author of "Ireland and her Churches," late Irish Correspondent of the *Times*. 8vo. 12s.

A History of the Irish Land Question. "There is probably no other account so compendious and so complete."—FORTNIGHTLY REVIEW.

Guide to the Unprotected, in Every Day Matters Relating to Property and Income. By a BANKER'S DAUGHTER. Third Edition. Extra fcap. 8vo. 3s. 6d.

Many widows and single ladies, and all young people, on first possessing money of their own, are in want of advice when they have commonplace business matters to transact. The author of this work writes for those who know nothing. Her aim throughout is to avoid all technicalities; to give plain and practical directions, not only as to what ought to be done, but how to do it. "Many an unprotected females will bless the head which planned and the hand which compiled this admirable little manual. . . . This book was very much wanted, and it could not have been better done."— MORNING STAR.

Hill.—CHILDREN OF THE STATE. THE TRAINING OF JUVENILE PAUPERS. By FLORENCE HILL. Extra fcap. 8vo. cloth. 5s.

In this work the author discusses the various systems adopted in this and other countries in the treatment of pauper children. The BIRMINGHAM DAILY GAZETTE *calls it "a valuable contribution to the great and important social question which it so ably and thoroughly discusses; and it must materially aid in producing a wise method of dealing with the Children of the State."*

Historicus.—LETTERS ON SOME QUESTIONS OF INTERNATIONAL LAW. Reprinted from the *Times*, with considerable Additions. 8vo. 7s. 6d. Also, ADDITIONAL LETTERS. 8vo. 2s. 6d.

The author's intention in these Letters was to illustrate in a popular form clearly-established principles of law, or to refute, as occasion required, errors which had obtained a mischievous currency. He has endeavoured to establish, by sufficient authority, propositions which have been inconsiderately impugned, and to point out the various methods of reasoning which have led some modern writers to erroneous conclusions. The volume contains: Letters on "Recognition;" "On the Perils of Intervention;" "The Rights and Duties of Neutral Nations;" "On the Law of Blockade;" "On Neutral Trade in Contraband of War;" "On Belligerent Violation of Neutral Rights;" "The Foreign Enlistment Act;" "The Right of Search;" extracts from letters on the Affair of the Trent; and a paper on the "Territoriality of the Merchant Vessel."—"It is seldom that the doctrines of International Law on debateable points have been stated with more vigour, precision, and certainty."—SATURDAY REVIEW.

Jevons.—Works by W. STANLEY JEVONS, M.A., Professor of Logic and Political Economy in Owens College, Manchester. (For other Works by the same Author, *see* EDUCATIONAL and PHILOSOPHICAL CATALOGUES.)

THE COAL QUESTION: An Inquiry Concerning the Progress of the Nation, and the Probable Exhaustion of our Coal Mines. Second Edition, revised. 8vo. 10s. 6d.

Jevons (W.S.)—*continued*.

"Day by day," the author says, "it becomes more evident that the coal we happily possess in excellent quality and abundance is the mainspring of modern material civilization." Geologists and other competent authorities have of late been hinting that the supply of coal is by no means inexhaustible, and as it is of vast importance to the country and the world generally to know the real state of the case, Professor Jevons in this work has endeavoured to solve the question as far as the data at command admit. He believes that should the consumption multiply for rather more than a century at its present rate, the average depth of our coal mines would be so reduced that we could not long continue our present rate of progress. "We have to make the momentous choice," he believes, "between brief greatness and long-continued prosperity."—" The question of our supply of coal," says the PALL MALL GAZETTE, *" becomes a question obviously of life or death. . . . The whole case is stated with admirable clearness and cogency. . . . We may regard his statements as unanswered and practically established."*

THE THEORY OF POLITICAL ECONOMY. 8vo. 9s.

In this work Professor Jevons endeavours to construct a theory of Political Economy on a mathematical or quantitative basis, believing that many of the commonly received theories in this science are perniciously erroneous. The author here attempts to treat Economy as the Calculus of Pleasure and Pain, and has sketched out, almost irrespective of previous opinions, the form which the science, as it seems to him, must ultimately take. The theory consists in applying the differential calculus to the familiar notions of Wealth, Utility, Value, Demand, Supply, Capital, Interest, Labour, and all the other notions belonging to the daily operations of industry. As the complete theory of almost every other science involves the use of that calculus, so, the author thinks, we cannot have a true theory of Political Economy without its aid. "Professor Jevons has done invaluable service by courageously claiming political economy to be strictly a branch of Applied Mathematics."—WESTMINSTER REVIEW.

Martin.—THE STATESMAN'S YEAR-BOOK: A Statistical and Historical Annual of the States of the Civilized World. Handbook for Politicians and Merchants for the year 1872. By

FREDERICK MARTIN. Ninth Annual Publication. Revised after Official Returns. Crown 8vo. 10s. 6d.

The Statesman's Year-Book is the only work in the English language which furnishes a clear and concise account of the actual condition of all the States of Europe, the civilized countries of America, Asia, and Africa, and the British Colonies and Dependencies in all parts of the world. The new issue of the work has been revised and corrected, on the basis of official reports received direct from the heads of the leading Governments of the world, in reply to letters sent to them by the Editor. Through the valuable assistance thus given, it has been possible to collect an amount of information, political, statistical, and commercial, of the latest date, and of unimpeachable trustworthiness, such as no publication of the same kind has ever been able to furnish. The new issue of the Statesman's Year-Book *has a Chronological Account of the principal events of the past momentous twelve months. "As indispensable as Bradshaw."* —TIMES.

Phillimore.—PRIVATE LAW AMONG THE ROMANS, from the Pandects. By JOHN GEORGE PHILLIMORE, Q.C. 8vo. 16s.

The author's belief that some knowledge of the Roman System of Municipal Law will contribute to improve our own, has induced him to prepare the present work. His endeavour has been to select those parts of the Digest which would best show the grand manner in which the Roman jurist dealt with his subject, as well as those which most illustrate the principles by which he was guided in establishing the great lines and propositions of jurisprudence, which every lawyer must have frequent occasion to employ. "Mr. Phillimore has done good service towards the study of jurisprudence in this country by the production of this volume. The work is one which should be in the hands of every student."—ATHENÆUM.

Smith.—Works by Professor GOLDWIN SMITH :—

A LETTER TO A WHIG MEMBER OF THE SOUTHERN INDEPENDENCE ASSOCIATION. Extra fcap. 8vo. 2s.

This is a Letter, written in 1864, to a member of an Association formed in this country, the purpose of which was "to lend assistance

Smith (Prof. G.)—*continued.*

to the Slave-owners of the Southern States in their attempt to effect a disruption of the American Commonwealth, and to establish an independent Power, having, as they declare, Slavery for its corner-stone." Mr. Smith endeavours to show that in doing so they would have committed a great folly and a still greater crime. Throughout the Letter many points of general and permanent importance are discussed.

THREE ENGLISH STATESMEN: PYM, CROMWELL, PITT. A Course of Lectures on the Political History of England. Extra fcap. 8vo. New and Cheaper Edition. 5s.

"A work which neither historian nor politician can safely afford to neglect."—SATURDAY REVIEW." *"There are outlines, clearly and boldly sketched, if mere outlines, of the three Statesmen who give the titles to his lectures, which are well deserving of study."*—SPECTATOR.

Social Duties Considered with Reference to the ORGANIZATION OF EFFORT IN WORKS OF BENEVOLENCE AND PUBLIC UTILITY. By a MAN OF BUSINESS. (WILLIAM RATHBONE.) Fcap. 8vo. 4s. 6d.

The contents of this valuable little book are—I. "Social Disintegration." II. "Our Charities—Done and Undone." III. "Organization and Individual Benevolence—their Achievements and Shortcomings." IV. "Organization and Individualism—their Co-operation Indispensable." V. "Instances and Experiments." VI. "The Sphere of Government." "Conclusion." The views urged are no sentimental theories, but have grown out of the practical experience acquired in actual work. "Mr. Rathbone's earnest and large-hearted little book will help to generate both a larger and wiser charity."—BRITISH QUARTERLY.

Stephen (C. E.)—THE SERVICE OF THE POOR; Being an Inquiry into the Reasons for and against the Establishment of Religious Sisterhoods for Charitable Purposes. By CAROLINE EMILIA STEPHEN. Crown 8vo. 6s. 6d.

Miss Stephen defines Religious Sisterhoods as "associations, the organization of which is based upon the assumption that works of charity are either acts of worship in themselves, or means to an end, that end being the spiritual welfare of the objects or the performers of those works." Arguing from that point of view, she devotes the first part of her volume to a brief history of religious associations, taking as specimens—*I. The Deaconesses of the Primitive Church. II. The Béguines. III. The Third Order of S. Francis. IV. The Sisters of Charity of S. Vincent de Paul. V. The Deaconesses of Modern Germany.* In the second part, Miss Stephen attempts to show what are the real wants met by Sisterhoods, to what extent the same wants may be effectually met by the organization of corresponding institutions on a secular basis, and what are the reasons for endeavouring to do so. "*The ablest advocate of a better line of work in this direction than we have ever seen.*"—EXAMINER.

Stephen (J. F.)—A GENERAL VIEW OF THE CRIMINAL LAW OF ENGLAND. By JAMES FITZJAMES STEPHEN, M.A., Barrister-at-Law, Member of the Legislative Council of India. 8vo. 18s.

The object of this work is to give an account of the general scope, tendency, and design of an important part of our institutions, of which surely none can have a greater moral significance, or be more closely connected with broad principles of morality and politics, than those by which men rightfully, deliberately, and in cold blood, kill, enslave, and otherwise torment their fellow-creatures. The author believes it possible to explain the principles of such a system in a manner both intelligible and interesting. The Contents are—I. "The Province of the Criminal Law." II. "Historical Sketch of English Criminal Law." III. "Definition of Crime in General." IV. "Classification and Definition of Particular Crimes." V. "Criminal Procedure in General." VI. "English Criminal Procedure." VII. "The Principles of Evidence in Relation to the Criminal Law." VIII. "English Rules of Evidence." IX. "English Criminal Legislation." The last 150 *pages are occupied with the discussion of a number of important cases. "Readers feel in his book the confidence which attaches to the writings of a man who has a great practical acquaintance with the matter of which he writes, and lawyers will agree that it fully satisfies the standard of professional accuracy."* —SATURDAY REVIEW. "*His style is forcible and perspicuous, and singularly free from the unnecessary use of professional terms.*"— SPECTATOR.

Thornton.—ON LABOUR: Its Wrongful Claims and Rightful Dues; Its Actual Present State and Possible Future. By WILLIAM THOMAS THORNTON, Author of "A Plea for Peasant Proprietors," etc. Second Edition, revised. 8vo. 14s.

> *The object of this volume is to endeavour to find "a cure for human destitution," the search after which has been the passion and the work of the author's life. The work is divided into four books, and each book into a number of chapters. Book I. "Labour's Causes of Discontent." II. "Labour and Capital in Debate." III. "Labour and Capital in Antagonism." IV. "Labour and Capital in Alliance." All the highly important problems in Social and Political Economy connected with Labour and Capital are here discussed with knowledge, vigour, and originality, and for a noble purpose. The new edition has been thoroughly revised and considerably enlarged. "We cannot fail to recognize in his work the result of independent thought, high moral aim, and generous intrepidity in a noble cause. . . . . A really valuable contribution. The number of facts accumulated, both historical and statistical, make an especially valuable portion of the work."*—WESTMINSTER REVIEW.

WORKS CONNECTED WITH THE SCIENCE OR THE HISTORY OF LANGUAGE.

(*For Editions of Greek and Latin Classical Authors, Grammars, and other School works, see* EDUCATIONAL CATALOGUE.)

Abbott.—A SHAKESPERIAN GRAMMAR: An Attempt to illustrate some of the Differences between Elizabethan and Modern English. By the Rev. E. A. ABBOTT, M.A., Head Master of the City of London School. For the Use of Schools. New and Enlarged Edition. Extra fcap. 8vo. 6s.

The object of this work is to furnish students of Shakespeare and Bacon with a short systematic account of some points of difference between Elizabethan Syntax and our own. The demand for a third edition within a year of the publication of the first, has encouraged the author to endeavour to make the work somewhat more useful, and to render it, as far as possible, a complete book of reference for all difficulties of Shakesperian Syntax or Prosody. For this purpose the whole of Shakespeare has been re-read, and an attempt has been made to include within this edition the explanation of every idiomatic difficulty (where the text is not confessedly corrupt) that comes within the province of a grammar as distinct from a glossary. The great object being to make a useful book of reference for students and for classes in schools, several Plays have been indexed so fully, that with the aid of a glossary and historical notes the references will serve for a complete commentary. "*A critical inquiry, conducted with great skill and knowledge, and with all the appliances of modern philology.*"—PALL MALL GAZETTE. "*Valuable not only as an aid to the critical study of Shakespeare, but as tending to familiarize the reader with Elizabethan English in general.*"— ATHENÆUM.

Besant.—STUDIES IN EARLY FRENCH POETRY. By WALTER BESANT, M.A. Crown 8vo. 8s. 6d.

*A sort of impression rests on most minds that French literature begins with the "siècle de Louis Quatorze;" any previous literature being for the most part unknown or ignored. Few know anything of the enormous literary activity that began in the thirteenth century, was carried on by Rulebeuf, Marie de France, Gaston de Foix, Thibault de Champagne, and Lorris; was fostered by Charles of Orleans, by Margaret of Valois, by Francis the First; that gave a crowd of versifiers to France, enriched, strengthened, developed, and fixed the French language, and prepared the way for Corneille and for Racine. The present work aims to afford information and direction touching these early efforts of France in poetical literature. "In one moderately sized volume he has contrived to introduce us to the very best, if not to all of the early French poets."—*ATHENÆUM. *"Industry, the insight of a scholar, and a genuine enthusiasm for his subject, combine to make it of very considerable value."—*SPECTATOR.

Helfenstein (James).—A COMPARATIVE GRAMMAR OF THE TEUTONIC LANGUAGES: Being at the same time a Historical Grammar of the English Language, and comprising Gothic, Anglo-Saxon, Early English, Modern English, Icelandic (Old Norse), Danish, Swedish, Old High German, Middle High German, Modern German, Old Saxon, Old Frisian, and Dutch. By JAMES HELFENSTEIN, Ph.D. 8vo. 18s.

This work traces the different stages of development through which the various Teutonic languages have passed, and the laws which have regulated their growth. The reader is thus enabled to study the relation which these languages bear to one another, and to the English language in particular, to which special attention is devoted throughout. In the chapters on Ancient and Middle Teutonic languages no grammatical form is omitted the knowledge of which is required for the study of ancient literature, whether Gothic or Anglo-Saxon or Early English. To each chapter is prefixed a sketch showing the relation of the Teutonic to the cognate languages, Greek, Latin, and Sanskrit. Those who have mastered the book will be in a position to proceed with intelligence to the more elaborate works of Grimm, Bopp, Pott, Schleicher, and others.

Morris.—HISTORICAL OUTLINES OF ENGLISH ACCI-
DENCE, comprising Chapters on the History and Development
of the Language, and on Word-formation. By the Rev. RICHARD
MORRIS, LL.D., Member of the Council of the Philol. Soc.,
Lecturer on English Language and Literature in King's College
School, Editor of "Specimens of Early English," etc., etc.
Fcap. 8vo. 6s.

Dr. Morris has endeavoured to write a work which can be profitably used by students and by the upper forms in our public schools. His almost unequalled knowledge of early English Literature renders him peculiarly qualified to write a work of this kind; and English Grammar, he believes, without a reference to the older forms, must appear altogether anomalous, inconsistent, and unintelligible. In the writing of this volume, moreover, he has taken advantage of the researches into our language made by all the most eminent scholars in England, America, and on the Continent. The author shows the place of English among the languages of the world, expounds clearly and with great minuteness "Grimm's Law," gives a brief history of the English language and an account of the various dialects, investigates the history and principles of Phonology, Orthography, Accent, and Etymology, and devotes several chapters to the consideration of the various Parts of Speech, and the final one to Derivation and Word-formation.

Peile (John, M.A.)—AN INTRODUCTION TO GREEK
AND LATIN ETYMOLOGY. By JOHN PEILE, M.A.,
Fellow and Assistant Tutor of Christ's College, Cambridge,
formerly Teacher of Sanskrit in the University of Cambridge.
New and revised Edition. Crown 8vo. 10s. 6d.

These Philological Lectures are the result of Notes made during the author's reading for some years previous to their publication. These Notes were put into the shape of lectures, delivered at Christ's College, as one set in the "Intercollegiate" list. They have been printed with some additions and modifications, but substantially as they were delivered. "The book may be accepted as a very valuable contribution to the science of language."—SATURDAY
REVIEW.

Philology.—THE JOURNAL OF SACRED AND CLASSICAL PHILOLOGY. Four Vols. 8vo. 12s. 6d.

THE JOURNAL OF PHILOLOGY. New Series. Edited by W. G. CLARK, M.A., JOHN E. B. MAYOR, M.A., and W. ALDIS WRIGHT, M.A. Nos. I. II., III., and IV. 8vo. 4s. 6d. each. (Half-yearly.)

Roby (H. J.)—A GRAMMAR OF THE LATIN LANGUAGE, FROM PLAUTUS TO SUETONIUS. By HENRY JOHN ROBY, M.A., late Fellow of St. John's College, Cambridge. Part I. containing :—Book I. Sounds. Book II. Inflexions. Book III. Word Formation. Appendices. Crown 8vo. 8s. 6d.

*This work is the result of an independent and careful study of the writers of the strictly Classical period, the period embraced between the time of Plautus and that of Suetonius. The author's aim has been to give the facts of the language in as few words as possible. It will be found that the arrangement of the book and the treatment of the various divisions differ in many respects from those of previous grammars. Mr. Roby has given special prominence to the treatment of Sounds and Word-formation; and in the First Book he has done much towards settling a discussion which is at present largely engaging the attention of scholars, viz., the Pronunciation of the Classical languages. In the full Appendices will be found various valuable details still further illustrating the subjects discussed in the text. The author's reputation as a scholar and critic is already well known, and the publishers are encouraged to believe that his present work will take its place as perhaps the most original, exhaustive, and scientific grammar of the Latin language that has ever issued from the British press. "The book is marked by the clear and practical insight of a master in his art. It is a book which would do honour to any country."—*ATHENÆUM. *"Brings before the student in a methodical form the best results of modern philology bearing on the Latin language."*—SCOTSMAN.

Taylor (Rev. Isaac).—WORDS AND PLACES; or, Etymological Illustrations of History, Ethnology, and Geography. By the Rev. ISAAC TAYLOR. Second Edition. Crown 8vo. 12s. 6d.

This work, as the SATURDAY REVIEW *acknowledges, "is one which stands alone in our language." The subject is one acknowledged to be of the highest importance as a handmaid to History, Ethnology, Geography, and even to Geology; and Mr. Taylor's work has taken its place as the only English authority of value on the subject. Not only is the work of the highest value to the student, but will be found full of interest to the general reader, affording him wonderful peeps into the past life and wanderings of the restless race to which he belongs. Every assistance is given in the way of specially prepared Maps, Indexes, and Appendices; and to anyone who wishes to pursue the study of the subject further, the Bibliographical List of Books will be found invaluable. The* NONCONFORMIST *says, "The historical importance of the subject can scarcely be exaggerated." "His book," the* READER *says, "will be invaluable to the student of English history." "As all cultivated minds feel curiosity about local names, it may be expected that this will become a household book," says the* GUARDIAN.

Trench.—Works by R. CHENEVIX TRENCH, D.D., Archbishop of Dublin. (For other Works by the same Author, *see* THEOLOGICAL CATALOGUE.)

Archbishop Trench has done much to spread an interest in the history of our English tongue. He is acknowledged to possess an uncommon power of presenting, in a clear, instructive, and interesting manner, the fruit of his own extensive research, as well as the results of the labours of other scientific and historical students of language; while, as the ATHENÆUM *says, "his sober judgment and sound sense are barriers against the misleading influence of arbitrary hypotheses."*

SYNONYMS OF THE NEW TESTAMENT. New Edition, enlarged. 8vo. cloth. 12s.

The study of synonyms in any language is valuable as a discipline for training the mind to close and accurate habits of thought; more especially is this the case in Greek—"a language spoken by a people of the finest and subtlest intellect; who saw distinctions where others saw none; who divided out to different words what others often were content to huddle confusedly under a common term." This work is recognized as a valuable companion to every student of the New Testament in the original. This, the Seventh Edition, has been

Trench (R. C.)—*continued*.

carefully revised, and a considerable number of new synonyms added. Appended is an Index to the synonyms, and an Index to many other words alluded to or explained throughout the work. "He is," the ATHENÆUM *says, "a guide in this department of knowledge to whom his readers may entrust themselves with confidence."*

ON THE STUDY OF WORDS. Lectures Addressed (originally) to the Pupils at the Diocesan Training School, Winchester. Fourteenth Edition, revised and enlarged. Fcap. 8vo. 4s. 6d.

This, it is believed, was probably the first work which drew general attention in this country to the importance and interest of the critical and historical study of English. It still retains its place as one of the most successful if not the only exponent of those aspects of Words of which it treats. The subjects of the several Lectures are—I. "Introductory." II. "On the Poetry of Words." III. "On the Morality of Words." IV. "On the History of Words." V. "On the Rise of New Words." VI. "On the Distinction of Words." VII. "The Schoolmaster's Use of Words."

ENGLISH PAST AND PRESENT. Seventh Edition, revised and improved. Fcap. 8vo. 4s. 6d.

This is a series of eight Lectures, in the first of which Archbishop Trench considers the English language as it now is, decomposes some specimens of it, and thus discovers of what elements it is compact. In the second Lecture he considers what the language might have been if the Norman Conquest had never taken place. In the following six Lectures he institutes from various points of view a comparison between the present language and the past, points out gains which it has made, losses which it has endured, and generally calls attention to some of the more important changes through which it has passed, or is at present passing.

A SELECT GLOSSARY OF ENGLISH WORDS USED FORMERLY IN SENSES DIFFERENT FROM THEIR PRESENT. Third Edition. Fcap. 8vo. 4s.

This alphabetically arranged Glossary contains many of the most important of those English words which in the course of time have gradually changed their meanings. The author's object is to point out some of these changes, to suggest how many more there may be,

Trench (R. C.)—*continued.*

to show how slight and subtle, while yet most real, these changes have often been, to trace here and there the progressive steps by which the old meaning has been put off and the new put on—the exact road which a word has travelled. The author thus hopes to render some assistance to those who regard this as a serviceable discipline in the training of their own minds or the minds of others. Although the book is in the form of a Glossary, it will be found as interesting as a series of brief well-told biographies.

ON SOME DEFICIENCIES IN OUR ENGLISH DICTIONARIES: Being the substance of Two Papers read before the Philological Society. Second Edition, revised and enlarged. 8vo. 3s.

The following are the main deficiencies in English dictionaries pointed out in these Papers, and illustrated by an interesting accumulation of particulars:—I. "Obsolete words are incompletely registered." II. "Families or groups of words are often imperfect." III. "Much earlier examples of the employment of words oftentimes exist than any which are cited, and much later examples of words now obsolete." IV. "Important meanings and uses of words are passed over." V. "Comparatively little attention is paid to the distinguishing of synonymous words." VI. "Many passages in our literature are passed by, which might be carefully adduced in illustration of the first introduction, etymology, and meaning of words." VII. "Our dictionaries err in redundancy as well as defect."

Wood.—Works by H. T. W. WOOD, B.A., Clare College, Cambridge:—

THE RECIPROCAL INFLUENCE OF ENGLISH AND FRENCH LITERATURE IN THE EIGHTEENTH CENTURY. Crown 8vo. 2s. 6d.

This Essay gained the Le Bas Prize for the year 1869. Besides a general Introductory Section, it contains other three Sections on "The Influence of Boileau and his School;" "The Influence of English Philosophy in France;" "Secondary Influences—the Drama, Fiction," etc. Appended is a Synchronological Table of Events connected with English and French Literature, A.D. 1700—A.D. 1800.

Wood (H. T. W.)—*continued.*

CHANGES IN THE ENGLISH LANGUAGE BETWEEN THE PUBLICATION OF WICLIF'S BIBLE AND THAT OF THE AUTHORIZED VERSION ; A.D. 1400 to A.D. 1600. Crown 8vo. 2s. 6d.

> *This Essay gained the Le Bas Prize for the year* 1870. *Besides the Introductory Section explaining the aim and scope of the Essay, there are other three Sections and three Appendices. Section II. treats of* "*English before Chaucer.*" *III.* "*Chaucer to Caxton.*" *IV.* "*From Caxton to the Authorized Version.*"—*Appendix:* *I.* "*Table of English Literature,*" A. D. 1300—A. D. 1611. *II.* "*Early English Bible.*" *III.* "*Inflectional Changes in the Verb.*" *This will be found a most valuable help in the study of our language during the period embraced in the Essay.* "*As we go with him,*" *the* ATHENÆUM *says,* "*we learn something new at every step.*"

Yonge.—HISTORY OF CHRISTIAN NAMES. By CHARLOTTE M. YONGE, Author of "The Heir of Redclyffe." Two Vols. Crown 8vo. 1l. 1s.

> *Miss Yonge's work is acknowledged to be* the *authority on the interesting subject of which it treats. Until she wrote on the subject, the history of names—especially* Christian Names *as distinguished from* Surnames—*had been but little examined; nor why one should be popular and another forgotten—why one should flourish throughout Europe, another in one country alone, another around some petty district. In each case she has tried to find out whence the name came, whether it had a patron, and whether the patron took it from the myths or heroes of his own country, or from the meaning of the words. She has then tried to classify the names, as to treat them merely alphabetically would destroy all their interest and connection. They are classified first by language, beginning with* Hebrew *and coming down through* Greek *and* Latin *to* Celtic, Teutonic, Slavonic, *and other sources, ancient and modern; then by meaning or spirit.* "*An almost exhaustive treatment of the subject . . . The painstaking toil of a thoughtful and cultured mind on a most interesting theme.*"—LONDON QUARTERLY.

R. CLAY, SONS, AND TAYLOR, PRINTERS, LONDON.

www.ingramcontent.com/pod-product-compliance
Lightning Source LLC
Chambersburg PA
CBHW020821230426
43666CB00007B/1052